Adoption and Foster Care

Adoption and Foster Care

Kathlyn Gay

—Issues in Focus—

ENSLOW PUBLISHERS, INC.

Bloy St. & Ramsey Ave. P.O. Box 38
Box 777 Aldershot
Hillside, N.J. 07205 Hants GU12 6BP
U.S.A. U.K.

Library of Congress Cataloging-in-Publication Data

Gay, Kathlyn.
  Adoption and foster care / Kathlyn Gay.
  p. cm. — (Issues in focus)
  Includes bibliographical references.
  Summary: Describes how these placement systems work and reveals
the feelings of young people who find homes through adoption and
foster care.
  ISBN 0-89490-239-3
  1. Foster home care—United States—Juvenile literature.
  2. Adoption—United States—Juvenile literature. [1. Foster home
care. 2. Adoption.] I. Title.—II. Series: Issues in focus
(Hillside, N.J.)
HV881.G39   1990   89-36476
362.7'33'0973—dc20   CIP
                                                                 AC

ISBN 0-89490-239-3
Printed in the United States of America

10 9 8 7 6 5 4 3 2 1

Illustrations courtesy of:
The *Elkhart Truth*: p. 103; Douglas Gay: pp. 69, 93; Kathlyn Gay: pp. 22, 27,
33, 36, 39, 45, 51, 58, 77, 83, 105, 110; Edna Ingram: p. 12; The Kaufmans: p.
26.

Acknowledgments

Many adoptive and foster families and representatives of groups involved with adoption and foster care shared information with me. I deeply appreciate their help, courtesy, and insights. Dozens of families opened their homes to me or allowed long interviews by telephone, taking time from very busy schedules to express with candor their fears and hopes, sorrows and joys, frustrations and special rewards in being part of a foster or adoptive family. Some families allowed me to use their names. Others requested anonymity, which I have respected. Since I cannot recognize all interviewees by name, I hope everyone who shared her or his views with me will accept this acknowledgment as a personal thank-you. And a collective thank-you to all who work on an individual or group basis to make families work.

—*Kathlyn Gay*

Contents

1

—

Those Who Wait

A colorful banner flew over the front porch of a modest house in a midwestern city. It read: "It's a Girl—Welcome Home, Sandy." But the newcomer being welcomed was not an infant. She was a teenager who, after the death of both of her parents, had been living with substitute families—three different foster families—until an adoptive home could be found for her.

Like thousands of other young people who wait for permanent homes, Sandy longed for a "forever family," but she had no idea that her dream would come true. She had some help when her photo along with a brief article about her appeared in a regular newspaper feature called "Sunday's Child." A single woman who had been trying for three years to find an older child to adopt was attracted by the photo and liked what she read about Sandy. That was the first step toward bringing Sandy and her adoptive mother together.

Who Waits?

Across the nation, many major newspapers run columns similar to the "Sunday's Child" feature that helped Sandy find an adoptive home.

Information for these columns usually comes from adoption books—loose-leaf notebooks compiled by private and public agencies that hope to place "waiting children" in adoptive or long-term foster homes. The notebooks are filled with biographical sketches like these:

> Joe, Native American (Sioux), born June 1977, is sensitive and creative but also a fun-loving child who yearns for a family that will provide encouragement, stability, and a home where his personality and talents can thrive. Joe loves creating things with paper and materials . . . is cooperative and helpful. He prefers to be alone and needs prodding to interact with other children.

> Michelle, born December 1977, and Deborah, born June 1975, both black, are sisters who need to be placed together with a one- or two-parent family. Both were in previous placements, including a foster placement, a residential placement, and an adoptive placement where they experienced abuse.

> Nasha, born October 1976, is of black/white heritage, a bright youngster who enjoys one-on-one contact with adults. She has normal or above normal intelligence but tends to be somewhat lazy in school . . . Nasha appears mature in many areas, but this can be misleading. Rejection by her birth mother and the pending move from her present foster home have delayed her in some social areas. She has been involved in counseling with the local mental health center . . . . The family will need to continue in counseling with Nasha to help her deal with residual issues of rejection and abandonment.

> Dawn, born March 1975, with blond hair and fair skin coloring, is an emotionally needy youngster and therefore is not good in team-related activities or competitive situations. Dawn is "boy crazy" and when around males she relates to them in inappropriate ways. She suffered severe neglect for her first seven years as well as abuse by her stepfather. She will need ongoing therapy to assist her with issues of violation and trust. It is preferred that Dawn be placed with a single parent.

These biographical sketches are usually accompanied by photographs.

Families who want to adopt can get an idea what the children or young people look like as well as read a little about their backgrounds.

Those who wait range in age from infants to older teenagers and may be living in the United States or in other nations, including Haiti, Costa Rica, Mexico, India, Vietnam, Thailand, Korea, the Philippines, Chile, and Colombia. A variety of private agencies in the United States specialize in finding U.S. families for children waiting in other countries.

Some of the infants who wait have been abandoned or turned over to child care centers because their parents cannot provide for them. Among the waiting young people are those who are mentally or physically handicapped or who have emotional and behavioral problems or learning disabilities. Others may have been waiting so long that many prospective parents consider them "too old" for adoption.

Differences Between Foster Care and Adoption

At any given time in the United States, several hundred thousand children are living in settings other than their homes of origin. That is, they are not under the care of their biological, or birth, parents. Substitute care is provided by workers—known as caregivers—in a residential center, in some type of treatment facility (such as for the handicapped or drug abusers), emergency shelter, or by temporary foster parents. Some waiting children may eventually return to their birth parents' home, but a vast majority need adoptive families or placement with long-term foster families.

Frequently, adoption and fostering are thought to be the same thing, but there are important legal differences. In the United States, a child in foster care is usually a ward of the court. A protective services or child welfare agency becomes the legal guardian for the child and takes on the responsibility of placing a child with a family or in an appropriate residential or treatment center. The purpose of foster care is to provide temporary around-the-clock care for children until they can return to their birth parents or be placed with an adoptive family.

Although adults responsible for foster care of children must perform most parental duties, birth parents still maintain legal guardianship of their children. In other words, they have some rights over their offspring. For example, only birth parents can consent to a foster child's marriage if she or he has not attained the required legal age. Birth parents must also give consent for minor children in foster care to enlist in the armed forces or to have surgery.

On the other hand, if a child is adopted, the legal guardianship of the child has been transferred by means of a court order to the adoptive parent(s). A biological parent can no longer claim rights over an offspring. Adoptive children "belong" to their adoptive families and have the same legal rights as do birth children in those families.

Laws to Protect Children

Young people become wards of the court for a variety of reasons. But the problems that lead to wardship fall into two general categories:

Edna Ingram of Laurelton, New York, always takes time to help her foster children with school work. Here she is shown with April and Gary Phillips.

1. Parent-related problems that range from parental neglect of children to physical violence in the home;

2. Child-related problems that include physical and mental handicaps, delinquency, or drug abuse.

In order for a child to become a ward of the court, he or she must be a minor and declared under state law a "child in need of services" (CHINS). Although state laws vary, they are patterned after federal statutes on CHINS, since some funds for state child welfare programs depend on compliance with federal regulations.

A section of Indiana family law, for example, states that a child may be declared in need of services "if before the child's eighteenth birthday . . . the child's physical or mental condition is seriously impaired or seriously endangered as a result of the inability, refusal, or neglect of the child's parent, guardian, or custodian to supply the child with necessary food, clothing, shelter, medical care, education, or supervision." Other provisions include endangering a child's physical or mental health; sex offenses against a child by his or her parent, guardian, or custodian; and allowing a child to take part in an obscene performance. The law also protects a child who is born with a drug addiction or suffers injuries, abnormal physical or psychological development, or a life-threatening condition due to the mother's addiction to alcohol or other drugs.

If an investigation shows that a child may need protective services, a law enforcement officer, probation officer, or social services caseworker may take custody of the child. The child may stay in an emergency shelter or other facility until a court hearing is held. If a juvenile court judge then declares a child in need of services, he or she becomes a ward of the court. As a ward, a child is under the supervision of a child welfare or protective services agency. Federal law requires that a child welfare worker prepare a case plan, which covers where the child will be placed "based on the child's special needs and best interests." The law also mandates that a child be placed in "the least restrictive family-like setting." Efforts must be made "to provide family services to the child, parent, guardian, or custodian."

Providing Services and Homes

Sometimes placement of children outside their family of origin can be avoided if there is economic aid or such social services as day care and homemaking help are available. For example, wage earners in a family might suddenly face unemployment and have no source of income. Help from public and private social service agencies in a community could ensure that the family gets through a crisis until new employment is found. Supportive services also might help families deal with alcohol and other drug abuse or care for disabled, delinquent, or emotionally disturbed children.

However, some parents refuse to use available resources or are unwilling to be caregivers. Parents may be unable to care for their children because of mental illness, drug addiction, or alcoholism. Frequently, such problems result in child neglect or abuse.

When out-of-home placement is necessary, child welfare workers may place court wards with temporary foster families or in some type of residential facility providing group care. Caregivers must make sure that children go to school at the appropriate time, stay clean, have proper medical and dental care, and behave in an acceptable manner.

The majority of adolescents and teenagers who have been in residential centers or in and out of various foster family homes for most of their lives want to be part of a permanent family. But the longer young people are "in the system"—in the custody of a state or private agency—the slimmer their chances for finding a permanent home. Adoptive parents usually prefer babies or very young children, although there are many heartening stories of older children or teenagers who have connected with adoptive parents.

Yet adoption may not be the most appropriate course for all children in protective custody. Some teenagers, for example, may still want to maintain a relationship with their birth parents and prefer long-term foster care until they are able to live independently. Perhaps a child has been with a foster family for a long period and would be damaged emotionally if placed in an adoptive home. Foster parents might then become legal guardians, established by a court order. A guardian can make legal agreements on behalf of a child. Although guardianship does not terminate birth parents' rights, it might provide the most appropriate permanent arrangement for some young people in foster care.

A growing number of children and teens who wait for homes need treatment for severe physical, mental, or emotional problems. But services for those with "special needs" are not always available because funds and staff are limited. These problems in turn lead to inadequate supervision and sometimes abuse of children in foster care.

TV shows and many recent news reports and magazine features have focused on the crisis and wrongdoing in the overburdened child welfare system. In spite of some failures in the system, however, "there are many more times when through teamwork, cooperation and hard work . . . the foster child or youth is able to return to an improved family situation or some other permanent care," said Barbara Jordan, a foster mother and awards chairperson at a National Foster Parent Association (NFPA) conference. She went on to point out some successes:

> I know personally a boy who was in foster care who will graduate soon with his master's degree. There is a young mother who spent a major part of her life in foster care, [and now] is successfully raising her own family and has been approved for a foster home license. We prepare many children for successful adoption and in recent years, the majority of children *have* returned home. Some time ago, the teenage son of a very hostile father was placed in foster care. After six months of creative, cooperative work by the foster care team, the boy was returned home. The foster mother received the greatest reward possible when the father put his arm around her shoulder and said, "The court took away from me a boy. You have given back to me a son." That is what foster care is all about.

2

—

Foster Care: Yesterday and Today

Foster or substitute care of children is an ancient practice. Early Jewish laws and customs required that minor children who were orphaned or whose parents could not care for them be reared by their relatives. As early as the fourth century, the Catholic church in Europe began caring for abandoned children, placing them in homes set up for poor and disabled adults.

In 1601, during the reign of Queen Elizabeth I in England, the first public laws were passed requiring the government to take responsibility for needy children. These Elizabethan Poor Laws, as they were called, set up a system to care for dependent children in mixed almshouses (poorhouses for adults and children) or through indenture.

The Indenture System

Indenture was a form of labor in which the worker was bound by law to serve another for a certain period of time. In exchange, a worker would receive food, clothing, and housing or other benefits. Many indentured people also became apprentices, learning a trade or craft while being servants. Young children who were poor, orphaned, or illegitimate frequently were placed as apprentices with craftsmen, called masters. The master craftsmen taught their apprentices various occupations and were responsible for their care.

Whether or not dependent children became apprentices, they were expected to be servants for the family until they could earn a living on their own. In short, this type of foster family care was seen as a business deal rather than an attempt to provide a nurturing family life for a child. Children in the system had little protection and could easily be forced into hard physical labor at an early age.

Indenture was widely practiced in England and other European nations and in America during colonial times, and it persisted through the nineteenth century. In fact, in the late 1800s, some 80,000 poor and orphaned children in England were shipped to Canada to work on farms and as domestic servants.

The indenture form of foster care and the system itself, which included many adults who were indentured servants, began to lose favor as North America and Europe became more industrialized. In the first place, there was less and less need for apprentices to do home-based work. Workers were needed instead for jobs in factories and businesses outside the home.

Another important factor in bringing about the decline of the indenture system was the amendment to the U.S. Constitution that banned slavery. Social reformers called attention to the fact that the indenture system often involved "involuntary servitude" and was like bondage. Thus it could be unconstitutional.

Reforms in Foster Care

Because of reform movements that were initiated in the mid-1800s, substitute care for needy children began to change. But there was little consideration at first for meeting individual needs. For example, the New York Children's Aid Society, established in 1853, placed more emphasis on protecting society than on providing services for what were called "vagrant, idle, and vicious street urchins" in the city. The society gathered up large numbers of homeless children and then sent them, in groups of thirty or forty, to southern and midwestern farms, which were thought to be morally sound environments. After their arrival in rural areas, the children were assembled in a town square, and farm families selected those they would take in. Some of the children certainly were treated like family members, but others served primarily as sources of free farm labor.

During that same period, private religious groups and public agencies in New York and other states set up orphanages—residential centers for children whose parents had died. But children in these orphan asylums, as they were called, were required to follow strict routines and seldom were allowed contact with their relatives. As a result, over the next few decades, some child welfare experts criticized the asylums, calling them too regimented and impersonal. The experts advocated more individual treatment of children.

Eventually Children's Societies that had been set up in a number of states began to recognize that substitute care should suit the child. Where possible, children were taken from orphanages and placed with foster families. Sometimes the stay was for several months, as with infants who needed the milk of a nursing mother. At other times children were placed with foster families just before adoption or as they prepared to go on to independent living.

Still, many people involved with child welfare believed that institutional care was better than placement with foster families. Not until the years following a 1909 White House Conference on Children, which emphasized the benefits of foster family care, did the large orphan asylums gradually close down. Although foster parents were considered the best substitutes for biological families, foster homes were not always available. So agencies placed children in smaller facilities, referred to as "cottage-type" institutions.

About the time changes were taking place in the foster care system, the U.S. Congress set up the Children's Bureau, which is now within the Department of Health and Human Services. Celebrating seventy-eight years in 1990, the Children's Bureau has long administered federal programs that deal with foster care and adoption. The bureau also administers a variety of child welfare services, including treatment centers for children with special needs.

Since the middle of the twentieth century, residential treatment centers across the nation have served children with physical disabilities and emotional and behavior problems. But there has been increasing public awareness that some young people in the child care system need multiple services—comprehensive care that treats the physical, mental, and emotional needs of a child.

Sometimes comprehensive treatment begins in a residential facility. But care by trained foster parents, which child welfare experts call foster family care, is still the preferred substitute for the family of origin. However, social service agencies emphasize that foster family care should be for a *planned* period, either short- or long-term. During that period, reasonable efforts should be made to help the birth family—through counseling or other services—care for their own children. If the birth family cannot be reunited, the experts say adoption or permanent placement in a foster family is the next best step for children in the foster care system.

Variations in Foster Homes

In earlier times, agencies placed children with foster families who provided free services. As a result, the agencies had very little supervision of foster children. Parents could point out that they were paying the costs and thus should have the final say in the kind of care they provided.

Today, there are still some types of free foster homes—informal arrangements in which the foster parents are relatives or family friends who plan to adopt their foster children. But most foster parents are under the supervision of child welfare agencies, are licensed by the state, and receive payment for a foster child's basic needs.

There are about 130,000 licensed foster families in the United States. The care these families provide varies, depending on the needs of children who are wards of the court. Some foster families, like the Williamses of Rutland, Vermont, care primarily for children with special problems.

Over the past two decades, Donna and Doug Williams have provided licensed foster care for more than sixty children, ranging in age from three weeks to seventeen years. The National Foster Parents Association selected the Williamses as the 1988 "Foster Family of the Year." While receiving the honor, the family was praised for working "especially well with the biological parents" of the foster children in their care. Described as "real team players," the Williamses also were recognized for the extensive training they received in foster parenting and for applying that training in their care of children with multiple handicaps and children who were abused or neglected or had become delinquents.

Some foster families, including those who do not belong to foster parent organizations, offer emergency care. In Chicago, for example, several families provide foster care under a program called Exodus Homes. Sponsored by five North Side churches, the Chicago program is designed to shelter homeless teenagers for anywhere from one night to several weeks or up to several months. The young people may be drug abusers, AIDS victims, or prostitutes.

Another type of emergency foster care for teens is the Cool Home Family Program under the direction of Interface Community, a private family crisis and counseling agency in Ventura County, California. Licensed foster families working with the program provide short-term care for young people ten to seventeen years old who need shelter for a variety of reasons. Many are runaways. Some need a "cooling off" period, a time away from their families while social workers help them get counseling and other services they need. More than 30 percent of those coming into this emergency foster care program have been physically, emotionally, or sexually abused.

Across the nation, families who are not part of special programs also may be licensed to provide emergency foster care. In addition, the families may take in young people or children for regular foster care. In such cases, a foster family may serve hundreds of infants, young children, and adolescents over the years.

One more type of foster care involves families who take in teenage refugees from other nations. For nearly two decades, many refugees have come from Southeast Asian countries, particularly Vietnam, Laos, and Cambodia. Because of the Communist takeover of these countries, hundreds of thousands of refugees fled their homelands. In some cases, young people were forcibly or accidentally separated from their parents during their escape. In other instances, parents sent their teenagers out of the country to find a better life.

The U.S. government allows the Lutheran Immigration and Refugee Services and the U.S. Catholic Conference to process the teenage refugees for emigration to the United States. The young people are then placed in states that have established programs for refugee children and adolescents whose parents do not accompany them.

A midwestern family, who include three birth children and a foster child, look over a photo album of pictures of foster chidlren who have been in their home.

How Foster Families Are Selected

In cities nationwide—as well as in Canada and in some European countries—an increasing number of newspaper ads, TV commercials, and ads on billboards and in flyers have publicized the need for foster homes. But before a family can be licensed to provide foster care, a social service agency usually completes a home study. Although the process varies with each state, social workers usually must inspect a family home for possible health and safety hazards. There must be adequate bedroom space for foster children, who may share a bedroom with same-sex children but must have a separate bed. Families also must be willing to discipline without physical punishment, which is legally prohibited.

Along with meeting licensing regulations for the home itself, foster families are expected to have certain qualities. Some of these were outlined by a southern California social service agency in a recruitment brochure:

> Foster parents need to be willing to participate with and encourage the [foster] child in activities which will assist in the development of social and physical skills, and educational achievement. The foster parent must be willing to allow the child to make his [or her] own decisions regarding choice of and attendance at religious services. The foster parent needs to be willing to participate with agencies in planning for the developmental needs of the child. The foster parent and all other persons living in the home must have the willingness to accept the child as part of the family.

A social worker usually interviews each family member to learn personal attitudes regarding foster care. The worker also explains that fostering involves adjustments and sometimes creates stress for everyone in a family. It is particularly stressful when foster children have developed personal habits and patterns of living that are different from a foster family's life style—a common situation today.

Not too long ago, children placed in foster homes were likely to come from backgrounds similar to those of their foster families. The children usually needed foster care because their parents were very poor or seriously ill. But in recent years the picture has changed. Child welfare agencies nationwide have been able to help some parents get the services they need to keep their families together. Thus, when a juvenile court judge does decide to separate children from their parents, the order usually comes about because the children have been severely neglected or abused, which in turn creates severe emotional and physical problems. As a foster parent in the Detroit area for nineteen years observed: "Kids coming into care today seem more messed up than they ever did . . . very hostile."

Another long-time foster parent in Michigan explained that new foster parents seldom realize they may take in a kid who is going to "poop and pee on the wall." Foster parents also may have to cope with children who at eight and nine years old eat with their hands instead of using utensils, who do not wash regularly, who are infested with lice and other parasites, or who steal and fight. Some foster children may be so malnourished that they suffer physical and mental disabilities. Other children may have been severely abused in their birth homes and thus may be extremely fearful and distrustful or angry and destructive.

The very nature of foster care—its temporary basis—can also cause problems for some families. Close ties may develop between foster parents and foster children. During the 1970s, child care workers advised parents not to make such attachments, but that advice has since been discarded as being unhealthy for the child. Now, the philosophy is to love and show affection and at the same time learn to let go.

Foster parents Russell and Esther Hoover in Michigan have observed that it is easier emotionally to say goodbye when foster parents understand and define their roles. They advised:

> We see foster parenting almost like a vocation. These [foster] kids are only borrowed—not ours to keep or hang on to. It's much like being a teacher—you expect to be dealing with them for an undetermined time. Some you can help, some don't want any help. So you give it your best shot—to be the best role model

you know how to be, make them feel wanted and cared about, listen to their hurts and disappointments—don't take their rejections too personally. And then let go when it's time again for someone else to take over.

Why Families Provide Foster Care

With all the difficulties and strains involved in fostering, why would families want to provide substitute care? There is a widespread notion that people become foster parents in order to "make money." Some families do see fostering as a way to increase their income. But the daily or monthly allotment, which varies by counties within each state, seldom covers food and clothing expenses for foster children. In addition, welfare agencies are required to check a family's personal references and income to see that the family is not depending on foster care allowances to meet its own needs.

One of the primary reasons families take in foster children is to increase their family size and provide companionship for birth children. In other instances, couples do not have children of their own and want to parent through foster care, which eventually may lead to adoption.

Another major motivation is the desire to be of service to children. A study of 115 new foster parents in Wisconsin, Minnesota, and Illinois pointed out that the vast majority expressed not only "some sort of child-centered interest or concern for children in need of substitute care" but also the desire to enhance their own family life.

Joyce Kaufman, a foster parent in Elma, New York, explained why she and her husband, Sol, first decided to become a foster family about twenty years ago. "I wanted to be able to use my education and also my experience working with handicapped children and still be able to stay home with our own four small boys," she said. "I liked the idea of working with a child on a one-to-one basis rather than in a large group, and I liked the idea that the whole family would be involved. I felt it would be an enriching experience for my own kids, too—which it has been. We also felt that we had already contributed enough to the 'population explosion' but we still wanted to care for, nurture, and love more children and foster care seemed the perfect answer for us."

That view was echoed by a foster family in Lake Bluff, Illinois, a quiet suburban area northwest of Chicago. Don, a teacher, and Sue, who says her "main role is being a mom and I enjoy it," are the birth parents of three children, Kimberly, Erica, and Philip. Don and Sue have found great personal satisfaction in being foster parents. They have taken in infants placed for a few days or weeks until they were adopted or returned to birth parents. They also have fostered several older children who stayed from a few months to over a year.

Their birth children feel they have gained from the fostering experiences too. As the eldest, Kimberly, put it: "I know I've grown from it. I love having foster kids here. I'm sure it will be something I will do when I have my own family. I've gotten a sense of where other

Sol and Joyce Kaufman with their adopted daughter Jessie and foster son Demetrius. Jessie is trying to hold "Cookie" the rabbit still so Sol can cut his toenails.

26

people come from and how they live and how good we have it compared to what the foster kids have had. Sometimes we complain because we don't get something or things don't work out as planned, but foster kids have it much worse. We have a lot to be thankful for."

Some parents take in foster kids because they feel they have a special understanding; they know what it is like to be removed from birth parents and placed in foster homes. Lindy Loyd, a foster mother in the southern Illinois town of Murpheysboro, put it simply: "I've been there."

Lindy went on to explain in a low voice, sometimes pausing to control her emotions:

> When I was a kid, I was in and out of foster homes. My dad was abusive and used to beat us—my two sisters, brother and me. We were in Chicago then. One Christmastime when my mom said she was going to leave my dad, he lined all of us kids on the floor under the Christmas tree, leveled a shotgun at us and threatened to kill us if Mom left. Another time my dad beat me up so severely

Lindy Loyd poses with her foster son, Dale Dorch, near a convention center where they were attending a National Foster Parent Association conference.

that I was knocked out for two hours. He left for work and my sister revived me. When I came to we had a family conference and decided that our dad would end up killing one or all of us. So I rode my bicycle across town to the Austin police station where I passed out again.

At the station, Lindy was befriended by an officer who had talked to the family many times before. He explained that Lindy would have to sign a report charging her father with abuse and then she would immediately go into foster care. "I was willing to sign the report but not until the police went to get my sisters and brother," Lindy said. "If my dad had come home and found out what I'd done he'd have killed the other kids. It was scary, devastating, because no matter what he'd done this was my parent—I was supposed to love and obey him—that was what I'd been taught—but he wasn't living up to his end of things."

Today, Lindy staunchly supports foster family care and the kids she takes into her home. She and her husband, John, who are the birth parents of one son, now include in their family four foster sons. The oldest, Dale, who is now a young adult, has nothing but praise for his long-term foster family, calling them his "real family." He will stay with them, he says, until he is ready for independent living.

3

Living in Foster Families

Call them Dan, Kate, Holly, Gail, and Charles. To protect their privacy, their real names cannot be given. All were teenagers, and all had been in foster care, one since she was a baby and the others for periods of from five to nine years. Under the direction of a child welfare worker, they had formed a speakers' panel to respond to questions from adults attending a national conference on foster care. Although it was not easy for the teenagers to be on public display and to allow others to probe their feelings, they answered the questions candidly.

Reactions to Foster Care

"How did you feel when you first went to live with a foster family?" was the opening query.

Dan was the first to reply. "I felt kind of alone. It took a while to get used to it. I didn't want to talk to anyone," he said.

Others on the panel expressed similar reactions:

"I felt lost," Kate said. "I was angry at first, then really scared and lonely."

"I felt trapped. I just wanted to get out," Charles said quietly.

"I felt scared," Gail said and paused before adding, "In a way I was happy to be out of the situation I'd been in. It's just hard."

Whenever foster children and young people can speak out about their feelings, they are likely to try to explain how hard it is to be seen or labeled as a foster kid—being different. "You get a lot of hassle from other kids at high school," one member of the teenage panel explained. "Kids put you down being a foster child—they think you did wrong. They think you're bad or your parents are bad. Sometimes they make fun."

Feelings of inferiority, worthlessness, anxiety, fear, loneliness, anger—these are common reactions to an initial placement in foster care. Besides coping with intense emotions, some young people who enter foster care for the first time also must face dealing with other foster children and/or the birth children.

Holly said she particularly resented a four-year-old (call her Annie) "who was spoiled rotten. Like, my foster mother did nothing when Annie hit me in the face. In fact, my foster mother threatened me—that if I hit Annie back or anything, she—my foster mother—would kick me out. Once Annie stole two dollars from me and my foster mother said it was my fault because I'd left the money out in my room."

Another group of foster youth, who had an opportunity to express their opinions in a public forum, pointed out that they also had had various difficulties with other children in their foster families. A report on their comments, prepared for the Child Welfare League of America, noted that young people in foster care resent the way they are "blamed for things that go wrong" and are expected to provide free babysitting for younger children in the family.

Another common complaint was the feeling of being left out, of not being a part of the family. Several youths in foster care said: "I want to be treated like a regular daughter or son," not just a boarder in a household. For some, however, a foster family does become like a biological family. As Charles explained: "It was hard at first getting along with everyone, but now I call my foster parents 'Mom' and 'Dad' and the younger boys—who are foster kids too—are my 'brothers.' I'd do anything for them. I feel we're like a natural family."

One of the most difficult aspects of foster care is having someone "put down my biological parents," said fifteen-year-old Kate. That view was repeatedly stated in dozens of interviews with foster youth. A seventeen-year-old summed it up this way: "I think foster parents need to know why I'm in foster care but they shouldn't force me to talk bad about my biological family. Like one family said they couldn't understand why I'd want to go back there—to my real family. I love my family even if they couldn't raise me right. Putting down my natural parents is like putting down part of me."

Although young people express hurts and dissatisfactions connected with foster care, they also recognize that foster parents offer love and are concerned about them. "Being willing to take me in is one of the most important things a foster family has done for me," one young man said. Another appreciated the fact that foster parents helped him get involved in sports and helped build his self-esteem by complimenting him on chores well done. One teenager was glad that her foster parents were willing to listen to her problems. Still another teenager said her foster parents had helped her to "control my temper and to understand myself better."

Many foster children and teenagers have stressed that understanding, expressions of love, and help with self-control are attributes of successful foster parents. But day-to-day living in a foster family (as in biological and adoptive families) puts these qualities and a number of parenting skills to the test.

Daily Living in Foster Care

No one description of a particular daily life style can be labeled "typical" of all foster families. Like biological and adoptive families, some foster families are rural or small-town residents. Others are city people. Foster families may be headed by single parents. Some may have above-average incomes, while others may be middle-income families. Occupations and professions of those who earn the income in foster families vary also, as do their religious beliefs and cultural heritages. Some families have been taking in foster children for twenty-five to thirty years; others are just beginning to provide foster care.

One family relatively new to fostering is the Breitzmans of northern Illinois. Margaret and Tom are the parents of two birth children and a foster child (call him Billy), all of whom are of elementary school age. Margaret's mom also lives with the family and is highly supportive of the Breitzmans' decision to provide foster care not only for Billy but also for newborns. The infants stay only a few weeks or months—until they are placed in adoptive homes or returned to birth parents.

"I particularly wanted to have newborns. I love the baby stage—I can hold them and cuddle them—and yet I don't have to put them through college!" Margaret explained with a hearty laugh, her enthusiasm for her foster care role bubbling forth as she talks. "We are licensed for kids from newborn to eighteen years old, but we decided not to take children older than our own. Billy is the same age as our daughter Katie, and the two of them are like biological siblings—sometimes they are best friends and play together well or sometimes they fight terribly."

Billy came to the Breitzman home because his birth mother has been unable to care for him and is working with counselors to develop a functioning, independent family. The birth mother lives with relatives and must establish her own home before the court will allow the return of her child. "Billy often says he wants to go to his own home and he visits his birth mother every week, but he doesn't seem upset when he comes back here," Margaret said. "He particularly needs the role model of a father and the closeness of family relationships. There appears to be very little affection shown in his birth family. It's great for him to have a grandma like my mom around, plus Tom's folks are nearby and come to visit often."

The Breitzmans have cared for Billy much longer than they had expected, and they are not sure when Billy will return to his birth mother. Although the Breitzmans well know that foster parenting means temporary substitute parenting, they are aware that the longer Billy stays the more difficult it will be to part with him. They realize as well that Billy may not return to a supportive, nurturing family or one that displays affection. But the only requirement set down by the court is that birth parents provide food, shelter, and clothing and a safe environment. "Only minimum standards are required," Margaret said. "The social worker told us that right up front."

"He may take steps backward in his development when he returns to his own home," Tom pointed out. "Sometimes that's hard to accept.

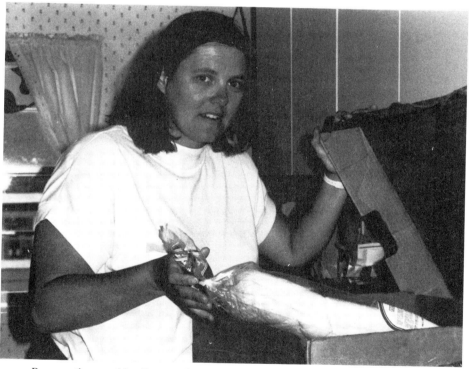

Because the monthly allotment for foster care hardly covers basic expenses, many foster families get help from local businesses. Here Margaret Breitzman opens a box of bread, pastries, and other "goodies" donated by a local bakery. Margaret will share the baked goods with other foster families she knows.

But we hope that the time Billy has with us will be of some benefit later in his life."

Foster Care in a Big City

Trying to provide positive experiences and role models for foster children to emulate is very much a part of the LoBello philosophy. Foster parents Marge and Vic LoBello are Chicagoans who live in a North Side neighborhood that is popular with up-and-coming professionals (so-called yuppies). The LoBellos, who are in their mid-forties, have redesigned and remodeled their two-story home as well as several rental properties nearby. Vic, a truck driver, is a talented carpenter, and Marge is an expert finisher who has "sanded more floors than I care to think about," she said. In addition, Marge has worked as a beauty consultant, providing extra income for their family of three birth and two adopted children plus various foster children who have been in their care.

One foster daughter, a teenager, has been with the family for several years and says she will "stay forever" or until she heads for college. As Marge proudly explained, "She's going to be a doctor. She's a straight-A student, third in her class, and will get a scholarship. She's already had the opportunity to work in Children's Memorial Hospital."

In the bright, airy living area, Marge, an attractive blond brimming with vitality, enthusiastically shows off framed pictures and photo albums of former foster children. There's a young man in a military uniform, a youngster with the look of a street fighter, a group of adolescents. . . .The finale is a family photo, blown up to poster size, Marge posing in front with wide-open arms, a gesture that clearly shows her welcoming, enthusiastic nature.

The LoBellos have welcomed more than two dozen young people referred by the Illinois Department of Children and Family Services. Most of the time, social workers brief Marge on the reasons the young people need foster care. Many come from the streets and are troubled, delinquent, abused, neglected, homeless, emotionally disturbed.

"You name it, they arrive with multiple problems," Marge said, adding that "sometimes you don't know what's happened to them. The kids won't say anything, but after a few days they tell me because I'm usually the first person to care and listen." Marge paused as if searching for the right words to go on. "I had a little girl once. I suspected she had been sexually abused, but I didn't know for sure until she complained about a rash. I was talking to the girl and I asked her when she had first noticed the sores. She told me it was at her own house, after an uncle who'd gotten out of prison had come to live with them and had lain on top of her. I took her to the doctor right away for a checkup. It was clear that the child had genital herpes. She was eight years old at the time."

The stories continue. Marge tells of young people who arrived without shoes and only the ragged, dirty clothes on their backs. A boy whose father was in prison and whose mother's drug addiction led to her suicide. A seven-year-old girl who had been sexually abused by her mother's boyfriend. A youngster who was going through such severe depression that just being around her "made me feel like I had a chain around my neck pulling me down," Marge said, pointing out that she tries to get therapeutic help for all of her foster kids.

Again the question arises, as it does for nearly all foster parents time and again: Why go through such traumas? For Marge, the answer is sometimes complex, sometimes simple. As she explained: "When a kid walks up those stairs, it's like he's been here forever. I feel that, and they feel that—they're relaxed. I know I can make a difference in someone's life. And that makes me feel great. In fact, when my husband comes back from a road trip, he always knows when there's a new kid in the house. I'm just bubbling about, acting like I've got a purpose in life.

Marge's "purpose in life" has its roots in her childhood. She, too, spent her early years on Chicago's streets. As she told it:

My father died in the war when I was a year old and for a while my sister and I lived with our grandparents. When I was about nine years old, we went to live with my mother. I can't remember a lot about that time, but it was horrendous. My mother was a drunk—a mean drunk—violent. We had to get out of her way. I remember being cold all the time and never really eating. We used to go to the movies and stay all day and eat food off the floor.

Many times the police picked us up off the streets and finally we were picked up enough that the child welfare department stepped in. I can remember going to court when my mother was charged with neglect. I had to testify against her—that she was bringing men in—it was terrible. You feel guilt, but at the same time feel shame for her, like you're telling on your mother, like a traitor.

After Marge's mother lost her parental rights, Marge and her sister went to live with their grandparents, who took custody. "We were

A television show featured the family of foster parents Marge and Vic LoBello. Here Marge looks over photos of foster, adoptive, and birth children in their family.

lucky," Marge said, adding that to this day she cannot understand how parents can get so far down that they will neglect or abuse their children. "Maybe that's why I try to be a good foster parent—take classes on child development, on sexual abuse, on drug abuse, all kinds of subjects that pertain to kids. I really get involved, which some people say is not good. But when a kid's life is on the line, doesn't know where he's going to be the next day, I go to court and nobody, including the social worker, knows about the case, I could go crazy. Kids need someone to stand up for them, to fight for them. It's tough being there for them, trying to keep them all going. Sometimes I say 'dear God, don't let me feel the pain,' but then I think if I get that sterile about it, that removed, why bother?"

Helping Foster Children Develop

There is no doubt that most foster families bother because they care. They believe that children—no matter what their troubled backgrounds—have positive attributes that need to be developed. Just such a belief is the basis for the foster care provided by the Miller family of Elkhart, Indiana, who have taken in more than fifty children over the years.

JoAnn Miller, who feels she has an innate as well as trained ability to deal with children, and her husband, Jim, an aircraft mechanic, began foster parenting in 1973, first in New York and now in Indiana. Members of the Mormon church, the family includes six birth children, two former foster children who have been adopted, and several foster children placed for short periods. Although there are usually two or three foster children in the home at any given time, that number increases as the need arises.

Nearly all of the children are of school age, so in midafternoon when a school bus stops on the road beside the Miller's modest home on the outskirts of the city, a small invasion takes place. There is a kind of pell-mell attack as the kids swoosh toward the door and bound inside, all yelling at once: "Hi, Mom!" "Guess what happened?" "See what I did!" "Look at this—I got an A on my paper!"

After reports on the school day are over, what next? "Ohhhhh," Joan groans. "You'll hear it." Someone begins piano practice, another starts on the clarinet, another on the trumpet. Music is an important part of family life, since as Jim explained: "We feel that music helps kids in their development and provides emotional release. And some of them have natural ability that needs to be brought out."

Another, smaller school bus arrives a few minutes later bringing home a dark-haired little boy, a foster child, from a special class for the emotionally handicapped. A victim of sexual abuse, the youngster hardly spoke when he first came to the Millers. He was terrified of older boys and men and frequently masturbated in public. But it is obvious, as the five-year-old joins the other kids in chatter and after-school chores, that he has made progress in establishing healthier relationships and acceptable behavior patterns.

Chores are an essential part of the Miller household routine. As JoAnn said: "I feel that children need to take as much responsibility as they can for their own environment. This is important for my birth kids and even more so for foster kids who may go back to homes where they have to take total responsibility for such things as personal hygiene and homemaking. We have a schedule that involves a major task such as dishwashing for a week plus daily chores for each child. Everyone's expected to do his or her part."

However, it takes more than cooperation to keep a foster family growing in constructive ways. Training in child development, classes in behavior problems, instruction on foster parenting—all help the Millers in their efforts to deal with children from family situations that would horrify the uninitiated.

"We are seldom shocked anymore," JoAnn said, "because we've had kids who have had so many terrible things happen to them." She began reciting some of the cases: Two young boys who lived and worked on a farm where there were no tools or machinery. "They literally dug out a basement with their hands. The boys at ten and eleven were so strong and tough—and mean. They had often been beaten on the head with a belt and with boards and sometimes as a form of punishment were not allowed to eat."

Then there was a young girl who at eighteen months old weighed fourteen pounds and who came to them with limbs broken and bruises all over her body; a seven-year-old girl who had gonorrhea from sexual abuse; a young boy who was practically starving. . . ."I can't help getting angry at what happens to some kids, although I never let them know," JoAnn said.

"Never, never, never," Jim emphasized. "To be successful, foster parents have to work with biological parents if at all possible. I know some foster parents who are more like ministers—they want to 'save'

The "chore board" is one way that JoAnn Miller keeps her large family of birth, adoptive, and foster children running smoothly.

the children from their natural parents. But that's not what fostering really is."

"Some children may not go back to the best situation but if they are clean and safe that may be all we can hope for,' JoAnn said. Still, the Millers have given many foster children a kind of strength that could stay with them through a lifetime: they have helped kids feel loved—unconditionally.

Sarah, the Miller's oldest birth daughter, is one of the best examples of how the family philosophy manifests itself. When in fifth grade, Sarah was asked one day to help a boy in the class who was shunned by other classmates because of his disruptive behavior. Sarah willingly agreed, and the teacher later showered Sarah with praise. But Sarah's matter-of-fact response was: "In our house we learn to accept each person because tomorrow he may be my brother."

4

Group Care

Some young people who come into the nation's child care system may stay temporarily in group homes or treatment facilities or for a long term in nursing or psychiatric centers. For example, parents of children with severe physical or mental handicaps may voluntarily place their children in institutional facilities because they cannot provide skilled care at home.

If children are removed from their birth parents and become wards of the court, child welfare workers usually study the available alternatives for care. Then they make their recommendations to the juvenile court judge, who determines the actual placement. In some cases, group care may be recommended because a worker has determined that a facility will meet a child's needs. In other instances, placement in a group care facility may come about simply because no other type of care is available at the time.

One of the most familiar group facilities is the group home within a community. Usually a group home is operated by or under the supervision of a social service agency. The agency owns or rents a residence and hires a couple to care for a group of six or so children who are in protective custody. Or the agency might staff a home with professional caregivers who are responsible for up to twelve children. Young people in group homes usually attend neighborhood schools, take part in community recreational activities, and in general function like members of a large foster family.

Another type of group care facility that has become part of many communities in recent years is the residential treatment center. Some centers focus on treatment for a single problem such as drug abuse, delinquent behavior, or emotional illness. Increasingly, however, residential treatment centers are becoming more comprehensive. That is, they are designed to provide multiple services to treat the whole child.

The Hope Center

The Salvation Army Hope Center in St. Louis, Missouri, is an example of a multiservices approach in a residential treatment program. The center began in 1977 as an emergency shelter for abused and neglected infants and young children. Now it provides a variety of services in a residence program that has treated more than 1,500 seriously ill or disturbed children from infancy to seven years old. According to the administrator, Susan Stepleton, the program ''is both humane and cost effective since it diverts children 'out of the system' before irreversible and permanent damage is done.''

Children and their families receive treatment and services from Hope Center staff trained in psychiatric social work, pediatric nursing, play therapy, family therapy, parenting education, and physical speech therapy if needed. Along with residential treatment, there is a separate facility for quality day care. In addition, a parenting education and therapy program helps ease family stress and thus prevent abuse and neglect. The center also has developed a therapeutic foster care program to serve children who are ready to leave the residential facility.

Staff provide intensive training over a six-week period for therapeutic foster parents. "During training, families hear many examples of the problems they may confront as foster parents. Staff members do not minimize the severity of the problem. They help families project the amount of disruption to their own family lives that may occur. The role of foster families as integral parts of the treatment team is emphasized and clarified," the director reported.

After completing their training, therapeutic foster parents also work with biological parents to reunify birth families. When reunifying the birth family is not appropriate for the well-being of a child, the center trains and counsels adoptive or long-term foster families.

The Children's Campus

Another comprehensive treatment center known as The Children's Campus is located in Mishawaka, Indiana, on a fifteen-acre wooded site along the St. Joseph River. Affiliated with the long-established Family and Children's Center Corporation, the facility accepts both boys and girls ten to eighteen years of age, some categorized as ''the most difficult,'' from all areas of the state. Young people are placed at the Campus because of such problems as delinquency, substance abuse, a history of running away, destructive behavior, or pregnancy.

Using a "Continuum of Treatment" approach developed by Campus Director Michael Puthoff, a team of professionals guides each child through a highly structured program to a less restrictive environment. "The goal," Puthoff said, "is to enable the child to work through life issues and emerge as an individual with a healthy self-esteem, a strong value system, and the ability to make appropriate and responsible choices. The multidisciplinary team coordinates treatment, and the same people stay with a child from start to finish."

Before a child is accepted for the Campus treatment program, a team of professionals that includes a counselor, school director, addictions specialist, campus life director, and intake coordinator determines whether the Campus program would be appropriate for the child. Upon acceptance to the program, each child is assigned a counselor who provides individual, group, and family therapy. A treatment team designs an individualized treatment plan for each child and on a weekly basis evaluates progress and recommends ways to meet goals.

Young people attend a Campus school, earning academic credits by meeting requirements of the local public school system. Some of the teenagers work in an independent study program to earn a General Educational Development (GED) certificate—equivalent to a high school diploma. Supervised school activities such as dances, choir, dramatic performances, team sports, and publishing a yearbook are all part of Campus life, too.

The Campus has a capacity for up to one hundred young people living in closely supervised cottages—single-story brick buildings, neatly kept inside and out. Splashes of color on posters, snapshots, and other personal items brighten the functional, dormitory-style rooms. Outside, the well-manicured grounds are accented with flower gardens and decorative walkways. But there is also a rustic quality. A ravine winds through the property, and trees and shrubs shield it from the nearby urban community.

Maintaining the beauty and cleanliness of the Campus is part of the treatment program. Residents learn individual responsibility by performing personal care chores. They also learn how to cooperate within a group by taking part in organized projects, in which young people work together to care for the living and recreational areas used by all the residents.

One of the major components of the Campus program is determining alcohol/drug history and providing counseling for those who are addicted. All residents receive extensive alcohol/drug education. Specialized treatment is also available for victims of sexual abuse and for adolescents who have committed sexual assaults. Psychological testing and psychiatric consultations are part of treatment as well. In addition, young women who are pregnant receive medical care, health education, and support during delivery. Counselors help teenage mothers maintain custody of their children or to place their infants with an adoption agency.

Making the Transition

Campus young people who are able to manage increased responsibilities begin to make the transition to community living. At first this may involve living under close staff supervision in a Girls' Group Home or a Boys' Group Home located in a nearby neighborhood. Group home residents attend community schools and usually find part-time jobs.

From group homes, young people may transfer to therapeutic foster care—a Treatment Foster Home. As with the Missouri Hope Center and other programs that provide intensive training for foster parents, The Children's Campus program carefully screens, trains, and continually supports foster parents. These parents will care for and guide the young people working toward their treatment goals.

Child care workers on the grounds of The Children's Campus, a residential treatment center in Mishawaka, Indiana, discuss programs for the day.

During the time teenagers are living in less restricted environments, they may also take part in another component of the Campus program: learning basic life skills. These include home and money management, searching and applying for vocational training and for jobs, and maintaining good nutrition and health practices.

Some young people, however, do not move smoothly through the phases that lead to less restrictive or independent living. As an example, a young man (call him Carl) had been assigned to a Treatment Foster Home and had visited the home several times. Carl had even helped one weekend to prepare his room for an extended stay. But after the weekend visit, the foster father learned that Carl had taken some cold tablets from a housekeeper and had stored the medication in his room. According to Campus rules, the act was punishable by a major loss of privileges, which would delay his placement in the foster home.

Although there are setbacks in some cases, staff at The Children's Campus can point to many "success stories." Here are a few excerpts, with names deleted, from Campus reports indicating that some young people are on their way to independent living:

> ———was placed with our agency at age 16. He was referred to us by the Probation Department for substance abuse and runaway. Prior to placement, this young man had been at a drug and alcohol abuse inpatient program for seven months.
>
> This young man basically had no family members who were interested in his treatment. His mother kicked him out and there was suspected abuse by his stepfather, who had adopted the youth, but then rejected him. He considered his dad and stepmother to be his parents, but there had been very little contact with them. His grandparents were his only visiting resource.
>
> He was hired at [a local fast food restaurant] after a lengthy interview. The manager praised him for his honesty about his past problems. Soon after being employed, he moved into the Boys Group Home. He completed his GED training and passed the overall GED test with very good scores. He had expressed

an interest in auto mechanics and was accepted at [a vocational school]....

. . . continued contact found that this young man had maintained his job . . . and appears to be doing very well.

18-year-old——was physically and sexually abused by both natural and adoptive parents. She spent four years in other residential placements where she had a history of running, and then was referred to The Children's Campus.

——'s first four months here were spent on campus in [a residential hall]. She then proceeded to the Girl's Group Home and remained there for six months. After progressing at the Girl's Group Home, ——entered The Children's Campus' Independent Living Program. She graduated from High School and is currently enrolled in beauty school training to become a hairdresser. She also maintains a job to cover her living expenses.

——progressed through our continuum of care spending her first months on campus and then moving to the Girl's Group Home. She received counseling for substance abuse and sexual abuse and responded very positively to her structured environment . . . She was placed in a Treatment Foster Home where she is currently excelling.

——is also in the Independent Living Program, so she is preparing for her discharge from the Treatment Foster Home. She has a steady job and attends regular high school where she is making positive, new friendships and working toward a college education.

Her stay in the Treatment Foster Home is giving her a second chance to have a normal teenage life. We feel this positive experience will make all the difference in ——'s future.

Helping young people become constructive members of a community is a major Campus goal. But success is not always measured in terms of whether a young person goes on to independent living. Some younger children successfully complete treatment and return to their families of origin. They are able to do so because the Campus program stresses counseling with birth families.

The counseling helps "young people see that it is not just one person in the family at fault, but the entire family structure is involved," said Campus Director Puthoff. "Our program is expanding. We are going out to the community where the child comes from, and contracting with an agency to provide counseling for the child and his or her family. There's a built-in support system so that kids aren't out there without resources."

Puthoff was quick to add: "We also attempt to teach the children about the resources they have within themselves—their mental abilities, their athletic abilities, what they've learned about applying for jobs and finding resource people in their community—all those things that may prevent them from reverting back to inappropriate behavior. The point is that we try to follow through with what is basic to our program: care, consistency, and structure."

5

Being Adopted

"I didn't really mean to take these two girls when the agency called me and asked me to come to Chicago to see them," said adoptive mother Martha Woods, a widow and licensed practical nurse living in Waukegan, Illinois. Martha explained: "When I got to St. Luke's Hospital and met the little girls, one of them asked me: 'Will you be my mommy?' I said 'yes' without even thinking about it. The little girls had been in the hospital for six weeks—they had been abandoned—left on a garbage pile—and were dying from malnutrition. Brenda, the oldest child, had two fingers missing. Later on, tests showed some brain damage, retardation, probably due to neglect and abuse."

The two girls joined Martha's family of seven birth children, most of whom have families of their own, and dozens of relatives in her extended black family of many aunts, uncles, and cousins. "I came from a beautiful family of twenty-three children," Martha said. "My father was married twice and when he married my mother he already had nineteen children. We were a happy family and we just love children so it's natural to have lots of kids around."

Martha is also the foster/adoptive mother of two boys, who recently were legally freed for adoption. As she explained:

> I took in Antwonne and Terrance as foster children several years before—but their mother would not give up her rights even though she did not want to care for them. Antwonne was really upset when I adopted the girls and could not adopt him and his brother. It was hard for him to understand because he didn't want to be with his natural mother.
>
> When he was younger, every time he went to see his birth mother, he'd come back and have nightmares and wet the bed and once threatened to go out in the street and let a car hit him if he couldn't stay with me. He thought I didn't love him even though I told him over and over again how much I loved him. He acted up and did poorly in school—mind you, now he's a straight-A student. But finally the birth mother's rights were terminated and Antwonne's behavior changed completely. Now he's a model student. He just wanted that security of knowing he belonged. Like he said: 'Now I can be a Woods.'

Creating a Permanent Family

Understanding the human need to have a permanent family has prompted many other foster parents to adopt their foster children, especially those who have been with the family for a long time and with whom they have developed strong ties. That has been the case with an Indiana couple, Bernard and Florence Veldman, who have been foster parents for dozens of young people since 1976. The Veldmans have adopted nine of their foster children, including several children from Vietnam, a black child with slight mental retardation, and a sibling group of three. In addition, the Veldmans are the birth parents of five children.

Although some of the Veldmans' children—adopted, birth, and foster—are out on their own, the household still bustles with activity, but at the same time, the home is orderly and has a peaceful quality about it. "I'm an organized person," Florence said with a quick smile.

"We work together as a family—everyone does his or her share and we support each other."

Besides always wanting to have a large family, the Veldmans say they "feel called" to be foster and adoptive parents. "We believe we are good parents and that God has given us the wisdom to raise children," Florence said.

"We also believe every child needs a home and has the right to be loved," Bernard said. "It hurts me to see children being neglected. So we began taking foster children into our home. But that is not enough. The foster children still know they are only here temporarily. But when we have been able to go to court to adopt them—what an amazing change. Then they know they do not have to leave. They are secure."

Enjoying a game is frequently part of the daily routine for large adoptive/foster families such as the Veldmans.

Debate Over Foster Parents Who Adopt

Although foster parenting sometimes leads to adoption, it is not the way that most adoptive families are formed. In fact, until recently, it was generally believed that foster parents should be temporary parents *only* and that foster children should be placed in what were considered "more suitable" adoptive homes.

Some social service agencies still see foster parents as mere "custodians" rather than people who can and do nurture and guide children in their care. As foster/adoptive mother Joyce Kaufman pointed out:

> More than one social worker has said to me, "You are the baby sitter, leave the rest to us." I've also been told that "most foster parents just take care of the kids. They don't worry about the future." Yet, our present foster child had five social workers assigned to his case before he was two years old. We had no consistent support or help from the child welfare agency—we were a "floating" case for months. Just recently, a new social worker finally was assigned. All concerned with our foster son's case believe his birth mother's parental rights should have been terminated long ago so that the boy could be released for adoption, but with the exception of our present worker, no one has been with the case long enough to follow through.

Some observers believe another factor in denying foster parents the right to adopt children in their care is the shortage of foster homes. If foster parents adopt, the reasoning goes, there will be one less place for a new child coming into the foster care system. But organizations such as the National Foster Parents Association and some adoption groups have helped establish state laws that require agencies to give long-term foster parents first consideration over other applicants, if their foster child is released for adoption.

An increasing number of agencies are taking a somewhat different approach to foster care by placing infants whose birth parents are expected to give up their rights with parents who will eventually adopt them. In other words, the prospective adoptive parents are foster parents for a time. This approach, sometimes called foster-adoption, helps provide a permanent home for a child right from the beginning. However, there is no guarantee that every placement of this type will result in adoption.

How Most Adoptive Families Form

Although there is a gradual move toward foster parent adoptions, the greatest number of adoption placements follow a more traditional pattern. Most first-time adopters are childless couples who apply to public or private adoption agencies. The couples want healthy newborn babies or infants a few months old who are like them in appearance and cultural background. But such adoptees are in short supply for Caucasian (white) couples. The National Committee for Adoption, a confederation of adoption agencies, reported that about two million white couples want to adopt the approximately 50,000 healthy Caucasian babies available for adoption annually. That is forty white couples per child.

The shortage of healthy white babies is due to such factors as the increasing use of birth control pills and legalized abortion. Also, as the stigma against unwed mothers has faded, an increasing number opt to keep their babies. Some feel the pressure of family and friends to do so. In addition, because of the high visibility of famous people who are single parents and glamorized media portrayals of single parenting, some young mothers ignore or do not realize the responsibilities involved in parenting. Thus, releasing a child for adoption may not be considered.

Some white couples who want to adopt through agencies have to wait years for a child—unless they decide to adopt an older child, a special needs child (a youngster with physical, mental, or emotional disabilities), a child from a cultural background different from their own, or a child from another country.

Adopting foreign-born children is one way that many white couples in the United States and Canada and some European countries increase their family size or become first-time parents. Those who adopt internationally usually do so through an adoption agency, paying fees that range from $6,000 to $10,000 or more to cover medical expenses, transportation, and legal work. Adoptive parents also must meet the requirements of the nation placing the children. For example, those adopting children from Korea must be at least twenty years older than the child and have no more than four other children when they adopt.

Most people who want to adopt internationally work with U.S. agencies that have long specialized in foreign adoptions. Such agencies not only help with the adoption process but also provide a variety of services for adoptive families after placement. Holt International Children's Services in Eugene, Oregon, for example, sponsors summer camps for foreign-born adoptees, ages nine to fifteen. According to the agency, the purpose of the camps is to help adoptees become acquainted with their birth cultures through a variety of supervised activities and to spend a week with other adoptees who are "just like me."

The Organization for United Response—usually called OURS—with headquarters in Minneapolis, Minnesota, and a membership of more than 12,000 in its thirty-eight state chapters, is the nation's largest organization of adoptive parents. OURS emphasizes international adoptions and publishes a bimonthly magazine that is packed with information to help adoptive families get the medical, legislative, and educational services needed for their children.

Many other national and regional organizations also provide information and services for international adoptees and their families. Addresses for some of these information sources appear in the list "Helpful Organizations."

Private Adoptions

Another way that adoptive families are created is through private or independent arrangements, in which an adoption agency does not place the child. In foreign adoptions, private arrangements sometimes can lead to serious problems and even tragedies. For example, because of the large American demand for foreign-born children to adopt, there have been numerous instances of baby selling. In some countries, "baby brokers" reportedly have persuaded poor mothers to give up their babies for foreign adoption in exchange for cash. Adoptive parents in the United States may then pay as high as $25,000 for a child. Some Americans who have expected to adopt healthy infants have found after placement that the babies have been very ill since birth.

Within the United States, some state laws prohibit private adoptions. In those states that allow the practice, adoption procedures must meet certain legal requirements.

Independent adoptions can involve stepchildren adopted by stepparents or children adopted by grandparents or aunts and uncles. In other arrangements, unrelated adopters may ask a religious leader, lawyer, doctor, teacher, friend, or acquaintance to help them find a birth mother who would like to place her child with adoptive parents. Some adopters place ads in newspapers, explaining their desire to adopt a child. An intermediary, such as a lawyer or doctor, may help place a child with an adoptive family. Or the birth parents and prospective adoptive parents may make their own arrangements.

For example, when Jane, a young Ohio woman, became pregnant, she wanted to have an abortion, but her family pressured her to carry the baby. Several months after her son Danny was born, Jane sought the help of a friend, Betterae, who often volunteered to babysit for Danny. She begged Betterae to take the child. Jane thought Betterae and her husband would make good parents. "Besides," Jane said, "I'm just not ready to settle down."

With guidance from an attorney, Betterae and her husband received legal custody of Danny, but they did not apply for adoption at first. Betterae felt sure Jane would want her son back. But months of custody turned into years in which Jane had less and less contact with her son. Finally, she relinquished her parental rights, and four-year-old Danny was adopted by Betterae and her husband.

Of course, not all arrangements go smoothly in independent

adoptions—or in adoptions through agencies. Before any adoption is final, there can be legal difficulties and long delays. Some birth mothers (about 10 to 15 percent, according to various estimates) back out of agreements and keep their children. A few who want to adopt decide they are not ready to accept the responsibility of raising a child. Some couples have marital problems and feel adoption would add to their difficulties.

All adoptions require some type of legal procedure, and those who adopt independently usually consult an attorney familiar with adoption law. In recent years, some lawyers have become actively involved in a controversial practice—advertising for and actively bringing together childless couples and pregnant women who want to place their babies in adoptive homes after birth. The practice is criticized because no legal standards have been set for such "matchmaking." In most states, only a birth mother or a licensed agency may place a baby with an adoptive family. An agency is able to screen prospective adopters through home studies, interviews, group meetings, and personal recommendations.

Lawyers who act as a matchmakers gather information on birth mothers and prospective adoptive parents, usually making videotapes of everyone involved. The lawyer also arranges for the parties to meet in person. An adopting couple pays the lawyer's fee for these services and also medical, legal, and living expenses for the birth mother. Critics charge that the practice is the next thing to "baby selling." However, couples who adopt through private agencies also pay adoption fees, and some public agencies charge for certain services.

If the birth mother chooses a couple to be adoptive parents for the child, the couple takes custody in the hospital. But after placement it usually takes six months in most states to finalize an adoption. As with foster care, state laws usually require that a social or human services department or a division of that department oversee the adoption procedure.

6

Joys and Sorrows of Adoption

After a child is adopted, a family does not necessarily live "happily ever after." Like all other families, adoptive families experience sorrows as well as joys, crises as well as triumphs. But there are special adjustments and stresses in an adoptive family, similar to some that are experienced in foster families.

When young children arrive in an adoptive family, they may be fearful and anxious, expecting their adoptive parents to abandon them as they believe their birth parents have done. Because of abandonment fears, children may be disruptive. One mother said that her adopted son "constantly acts out with destructive behavior because he was literally abandoned by his birth mother and now apparently wants to test and test us to see whether we'll keep him no matter what he does."

Many adjustments may be needed in families who adopt children with special needs. For example, in an article for *OURS*, one adoptive mother described her experiences with a six-year-old adopted daughter who had been sexually and physically abused by her biological father. The child now "survives with rage and manipulation," the mother wrote.

In spite of therapy sessions, extended family support, positive parenting, and love, the mother experienced daily traumas. She had to deal with her adopted daughter's temper tantrums, lying, and destructive acts. The mother also reported that her daughter has "nightmares that last for hours, in which I watch my little girl writhing in pain, uttering primal screams, sobbing, and unable to let me near enough to comfort her. She punches, kicks, and growls, fearful of human contact." Still, after six months of frustrations, and painfully slow progress, the mother observes that "life is a series of tiny steps" and that she and her daughter "go forward struggling. Sometimes, we even hold hands."

Fathers play an important part in helping adopted children overcome fears and anxieties. Here Jim Miller shows his children how to carve a pumpkin for Halloween.

What about older adopted children? Some, particularly those who have been in and out of foster homes or residential centers, mistrust adults and resist bonding, or closeness, even though they are in particular need of love and security. As adoptive parent and author Lois Gilman explained in *The Adoption Resource Book*:

> Children who move into adoptive situations need to work through their experience of separation. Whether they are separated from their foster parents, birth parents, or a caretaker in an orphanage, they will have to come to terms with what has happened to them before they can fully make new attachments. They will need help to open up, to talk about and share their feelings. The process of separation, and building new attachments, will be gradual and can take years.

Open Adoptions

As adoptees deal with adjustment difficulties, they also could be struggling with questions about their birth parents and their biological roots. Until about the mid-1900s, great secrecy surrounded North American adoption—in both the United States and Canada. Most states and provinces required that adoption records be sealed. The laws were designed to protect the privacy of any adoptee who might have been born out of wedlock, which in the past brought more social disapproval than it does today. There was also widespread belief that the laws would allow birth mothers to go on with their lives and the adoptive family to function like a biological family. As a result, adoptive parents seldom discussed adoption with their adopted children, or with anyone else for that matter.

But the desire to find one's roots in order to identify with one's heritage is a common human need, and some adoptees want to fulfill that need. In fact, since the midcentury, adult adoptees along with social service agencies have helped create a movement toward "open adoptions." In open adoptions, adoptive families have contact—sometimes anonymously, other times face to face—with the biological families of their adopted children.

When there is communication between birth parents and adoptive parents, information can be exchanged. Birth parents, for example, can provide adoptive parents with family medical histories and perhaps family photos and can discuss some of the reasons for releasing a child for adoption. Later on, the adoptive families can share this information with their adopted children, providing that needed link to their heritage and an honest response to the question: "Where do I come from?" At the same time, adoptive parents can share information about themselves in order to help birth parents deal with the emotional trauma of transferring their child to another family.

Usually open adoptions involve only one or two meetings between the birth mother and the adoptive parents. But a few social service agencies are helping birth parents and adoptive parents stay in touch, so that there is continual contact. Catholic social service agencies appear to be taking the lead in establishing open adoption practices. One agency, the Community Family and Children's Services in Traverse City, Michigan, has completed more than 150 open adoptions.

Pregnant women who come to the agency and request open adoption are able to choose adoptive parents from profiles—information and photos of couples—that the agency maintains. They may also arrange for continual personal contact with the adopted child.

Some adoptive parents become closely aligned with a birth mother, going with her during her pregnancy to doctor's appointments and to the hospital at the time of delivery. This practice, social workers and participants say, provides emotional support for the birth mother and allows the adoptive parents to share in some aspects of the pregnancy and birth experience.

However, there are critics of open adoption. Some point out that the practice is too new to draw any conclusions about positive or negative effects on the young adoptees involved. Since long-term studies on openly adopted children cannot be completed until the late 1990s, critics say agencies are really experimenting with children's lives.

Searching for Birth Parents

Many adoptees, particularly those adopted a generation or more ago, never had the choice of linking with their birth families at an early age. But some adult adoptees have been directly involved in organized efforts to search for birth parents. Adoptees have created networks and registries for those who want to get in touch with birth parents and vice versa.

The first U.S. search organization, Orphan Voyage, was founded in 1953. Since then other search organizations have been established in North America as well as in England and other Western countries. However, only about 2 percent of the estimated six million adoptees in the United States search for birth parents. Usually these adoptees are in their twenties or thirties before they begin a search, although sometimes they are adolescents.

The search, or just the suggestion of it, can cause stress in some adoptive families if parents believe the search has been prompted because their adopted children do not love them or want to leave them. But this is seldom the reason for wanting to find birth parents, say organized search groups, some child development experts, and many adult adoptees.

A search may be started because an adoptee wants knowledge about her or his medical history or inherited physical and personality traits. As one adult adoptee from southern Indiana explained: "I knew I had Welsh and German heritage, but as a kid I always wondered about my dark skin coloring. After I met my birth mother, I found out more about my biological family. It seems that the side of the family of German descent had quite dark complexions. I also wondered about my great desire to be on stage and to participate in amateur theater groups. Although there may be no connection, it was rather interesting to learn that I had a biological grandmother who was rather talented in what was then called 'elocution'—she gave dramatic readings."

No matter how important the knowledge of inherited traits may be, a search for birth parents usually is prompted by much more pressing questions. "Who is my mother? Why did she give me away? Who am I?" For some adoptees there is an overwhelming need to know the answers, wrote Clare Marcus, an adult adoptee in Canada who searched many years for her birth family, eventually finding them in Wales. Describing her experiences and those of many other adoptees in a book entitled *Who Is My Mother?*, she pointed out that those who begin to search "do so because of a strong need . . . to put faces to shadowy parent figures, to reconcile the past with the present, and to feel themselves connected to a normal historical continuity. . . .The moment of decision may come with some major life change: the birth of a child, loss of a child, death of the adoptive parents, marriage, or old age and the knowledge that time is running out."

In many instances, secrecy still surrounds the adoption process and adds to any turmoil an adoptee might suffer. As Clare Marcus wrote:

> I am convinced that the freedom to know, to take charge of one's own life, must become the absolute right of every adopted adult. I am equally convinced that everyone—birth parents, adoptive parents and the adoptee—will benefit from bringing adoption out from behind the wall of secrecy into the light of open understanding and honesty. I know, too . . . that some parents will not agree with me. Nevertheless, opening birth records to adult adoptees is . . . the humane way . . . the respectful and decent way to treat those adoptees who need to know about their origins.

On the other hand, it is not unusual for adoptees to say they have no interest in learning about their biological roots, except for medical histories. Some adoptees also fear that a search would lead to some unpleasantness and possibly traumatic experiences. Adoptees may locate birth parents who do not meet their expectations. "They may be real jerks," as one adoptee put it. Or the birth parents could make unreasonable claims on adoptees and create problems for a lifetime.

Some adoptees have found birth parents who are hostile and do not want to see them. Perhaps the birth parents have never wanted to have children and do not think of the relinquished children as their own. Adoptees might also be rejected by birth parents who feel guilty, ashamed, or remorseful or believe they will be hated for their past actions.

Does Adoption Create Psychological Problems?

Whether or not older adoptees search for their biological origins, some say they lack a sense of completeness and sometimes feel like "second-class citizens." A few studies have suggested that adoptees suffer emotional problems related to their adoption and carry this "psychological burden" for most of their lives. One study by Rutgers University psychologist David Brodzinsky links some adoptees' behavioral difficulties to grief over the loss of their birth parents and the loss of part of themselves. Adoptees may also carry feelings of guilt that they were "not quite good enough" for their birth parents to keep them.

Yet Brodzinsky has pointed out that the majority of adoptees "do very well in life," and some adoption experts insist there is no reliable data to support the conclusion that just being adopted is at the root of psychological problems. Other factors may be at work, such as the tendency of many adoptive parents to seek professional help—therapy, counseling, medical advice, and so on—as soon as behavior problems with their children arise. This gives the impression that adoptees have more emotional disturbances than the general population of children.

Another factor that may play a part in any emotional turmoil is the general negative attitudes about adoption that prevail in society. Indeed, the terms surrounding adoption procedures immediately suggest that those involved are somehow tainted. For example, a birth mother is said to have "*given up* a child for adoption." The statement suggests abandonment rather than the more positive act of providing a family for a child whose birth parents are unable to provide for his or her basic needs. Negative attitudes about adoption also are reflected in the insensitive statements of those who see adoptees as "poor little waifs" who are "lucky" to have been rescued. Or adoptees might be crassly told that they are "not the real children" in a family, leaving the distinct impression that they are somehow substitute, unnatural people.

Even adoptive parents may unwittingly pass on negative attitudes about adoption by denying the fact that an adoptive family is different from a biological family. As many multiracial and multicultural families have learned, the key to healthier relationships and stronger families is celebrating differences. They do not try to fit into a particular mold that the dominant society has established as the "ideal" family structure.

Angela, a teenage adoptee from Korea, who has been part of a multiracial/multicultural family since she was five, put it bluntly: "A person who's adopted can't always compare her situation to other people—like saying: 'I don't have parents who are really mine.' If you put yourself in that position, then you're going to feel like you don't really belong, like a reject. I don't remember ever having those feelings. I have just always tried to be myself—that's the way Mom and Dad have taught everyone in our family."

7

Children With Special Needs

- In Piedmont, California, the family of Bob and Dorothy DeBolt includes fourteen adopted children and six birth children. Of the fourteen who have been adopted, most are "physically challenged," as Dorothy DeBolt has described them. Some are blind, some are paraplegic, and others are emotionally scarred refugees from wars in Vietnam and Korea—in other words, young people with special needs, not the least of which is the need for a permanent family. The Debolts have successfully brought out the best in their children, raising them to be independent and self-sufficient. As a result, the DeBolts have been asked to help other adoptive families and have founded Aid in Adoption of Special Kids (AASK). Through the organization, more than 2,700 children with special problems have found loving, permanent homes.

- In Columbus, Ohio, the family of bachelor Kojo Odo

includes thirty-five adopted children, seven of whom are living on their own. Twenty-one sons and seven adopted daughters share Odo's ten-bedroom home, and all have been special adoptions—kids nobody else wanted. They had suffered abuse, had been abandoned, or were emotionally disturbed. Many are physically challenged, a term Odo, like the DeBolts, prefers over the negative "handicapped." An administrator for special adoptions in his state, Odo had always planned to adopt children when he married. But he remained single, and two decades ago when he applied to adopt a child, social service agencies did not think it was appropriate for a single African-American man to be an adoptive parent. After years of working to achieve his goal, he was able to adopt his first child in 1973 and since then has helped members of his large family achieve. As Odo explained to an Associated Press reporter: "I think [all kids have] the potential to do more than they have done. If we give them the vehicle—that's all I've been—they'll make use of it."

- In the small town of Dawson, Minnesota, the family of Roger and Pamela Reinert includes two birth children and seven adopted children. Again, the adopted children have special needs—physical and mental limitations or emotional problems—or have been considered "unadoptable" because they are older or there are no "matching" parents for their particular ethnic backgrounds. The Reinert's involvement with adoption of special needs children led them to establish a regional adoption agency known as Building Families Through Adoption (BFTA), which serves a five-state area and specializes in finding homes for "waiting children."

- In rural Cabot, Vermont, the family of Susan and Hector Badeau includes two birth children and eleven adopted children—whites, African-Americans, Mexican-Americans, a child from El Salvador, and another from India. Like other families who adopt special needs children, the Badeaus raise and nurture kids with varied physical disabilities and emotional problems. Some of the children had been in residential treatment centers, living in a group home where the Badeaus were once house parents. Because of their experiences with special needs children, the Badeaus founded an adoption agency, which they call Rootwings Ministries. It is based on their belief that children need ''roots to grow and wings to become independent.''

Many other families similar to those just described adopt children with special needs. But thousands of American children and young people labeled ''hard to adopt'' still wait for permanent homes. Some child welfare experts call it a national disgrace. However, only in recent years has there been widespread public information about waiting children. Those with special needs who became wards of the court usually stayed in institutions—out of sight and out of the public consciousness. Even as public awareness of special children grew, only a few foster or adoptive parents were prepared or felt able to handle severe physical, mental, or emotional problems.

Help for Families

Recognizing the need for training, some parents have taken it upon themselves to become informed. They seek out and attend workshops or seminars held in community hospitals, clinics, and mental health centers. In addition, child welfare agencies, and national, state, and local foster and adoptive parent associations have increased their efforts to provide training for those who will care for special needs children. Some training programs include on-site guidance. For example, a residential social worker from a child welfare agency goes to the home for up to thirty hours per week and helps a family use behavior modification techniques with children who are mentally and emotionally handicapped.

A National Adoption Center study, which was funded by the U.S. Department of Health and Human Services, found that parents who are willing to adopt special needs children are more likely to accept physically and emotionally disabled children than mentally retarded children. As a result, many children with varying degrees of mental retardation who become wards of the court may be placed in residential or treatment centers for long periods to await placement in foster or adoptive homes.

An African-American woman who has almost made a career of taking in "special ed kids" is foster mother Edna Ingram of Laurelton, New York. A widow and mother of three birth children, Ingram has provided foster care for dozens of children, ranging in age from four to fifteen years. All but three of the children need some form of special education. At the same time, Ingram has worked toward her college degree, placing on the dean's list. After graduation, she hopes to enter one of the four fields in which she has accumulated credits: social work, counseling, therapy, or special education. However, she applies much of her education and training on a daily basis at home with and for her foster children.

"Advocacy for special education children is what I'm about," Ingram said emphatically. She explained that "special kids who are in foster care need advocates, otherwise they may not get the kind of individual education or services that are available for them or should be available as required by federal law (PL 94-142)." Ingram noted that she has spent a great deal of her spare time—whenever she can find it—holding workshops on special education for foster parents in the New York City area and also for foster parent conferences.

As Ingram pointed out, many foster parents have not been informed of the federal laws regarding provisions for special needs children in their care. Even though child welfare agencies are legally responsible for children who have become wards of the court, they do not have regular contact with the foster children they have placed in homes. Sometimes welfare agencies do not have adequate background information about a foster child's mental retardation. This is also true in many adoptive placements.

Whatever a child's special needs, it is necessary to identify the handicapping condition in order for the child to be eligible for special services, which include an individual education plan (IEP). One requirement of the federal law, which must be implemented by the states, is that a public school system set up a multidisciplinary team to create an IEP for a special needs child.

Federal law also requires that handicapped students be educated in the least restrictive environment possible—that is, an environment in which handicapped children can interact as much as they are able with nonhandicapped peers. Integrating special needs children with

A mother helps her special needs adopted son understand a bank statement.

nonhandicapped children is often called "mainstreaming." Usually, a handicapped child's educational plan includes the types of mainstreaming activities or regular education classes that he or she should attend.

Barriers to Special Services

Even though the laws and regulations are on the books, schools do not always comply. Foster and adoptive parents complain that school boards are reluctant to provide special services. Both foster and adoptive parents in many parts of the nation say they have waited months to get appropriate educational placement for their special needs children. Some have been told that their school districts did not have the funds to pay for the special services required—not a valid reason for denying services, according to federal law. Other parents have encountered teachers who are poorly trained and insensitive to children with special needs.

Foster parents seem to face additional problems with school personnel who see them as "mere babysitters" because they have only custody, not legal guardianship, of special needs children. They also express their frustrations with social workers who do not take the lead in requesting evaluation and services for their children. One Colorado foster mother said she had "never known a teacher and social worker to get together" in regard to her foster children's special education needs.

But social workers argue that their heavy caseloads limit the time and energy they can spend with any child placed in a foster family. An Arkansas social worker said another problem is that parents "don't let me know" when there are difficulties at school but "wait until a child is suspended or there is some other crisis."

Advocates for Children

Both social workers and foster parents agree that they need to have good communication in order to work effectively for any special child's best interests. A Michigan social worker explained that he has had the most success with the educational placement and services for special needs children when he and the foster parents worked as a team. "We go to the first planning meeting together as advocates for the child," he said. "It takes a lot less effort to say to foster parents 'let's go to the school and work this out together' than to have the parents go several times to the school without results and I have to follow up time and again."

The team effort also motivates foster parents to become more involved in the educational plans for their special needs children. According to experienced foster parents, if they learn about the educational plans and related services such as speech therapy, counseling, and audiology that must be provided for handicapped students, they can urge social workers, who are the legal guardians, to act with them on behalf of their special needs children.

Another effective tool for many foster parents—as well as adoptive and biological parents of special children—is to write letters urging that appropriate services be provided for children's special needs. The more informed parents become, the more confident and assertive they are likely to be in seeking help.

While some parents work to meet the needs of mentally retarded youngsters, other foster and adoptive parents care for children with severe physical disabilities. Many such children have been in hospitals or nursing homes for most of their lives. A newsletter for members of Building Families Through Adoption reported how one man adopted an institutionalized child with severe disabilities:

> John Murphy, a 50-year-old court reporter from Chicago's Beverly neighborhood, first learned about Terry in the *Chicago Sun-Times* "Monday's Child" newspaper series. The article described Terry's availability for adoption, as well as his having cerebral palsy and living in a central Illinois nursing home. "What captured my eye was the T-shirt Terry wore in the photos," Mr. Murphy explained. "It was almost exactly like one in my wardrobe."
>
> "The twin T-shirt sparked Mr. Murphy's interest in Terry. But it was after several visits with this child, and immediate paternal bonding, that Mr. Murphy began proceedings for a legal

adoption," explained Becky Dunlavey, a social worker with the Lutheran Child and Family Services agency who aided Mr. Murphy in his efforts.

For two years and nine months, John Murphy drove 360 miles each week to visit Terry at his nursing center in Canton, IL. Although severely brain-damaged and legally blind, Terry did respond to Mr. Murphy's attention, according to Karen Baker, Terry's dedicated social worker at the Illinois Department of Children and Family Services. Finally, $3\frac{1}{2}$ years after beginning proceedings, John Murphy succeeded in adopting Terry. . . .[He was] moved to the Chicago Augustana Center, a skilled pediatric center . . . where his dad can more easily visit his new son as well as bring him home on weekends.

Even though Terry has an adoptive father, an increasing number of children with severe medical problems are being left in nursing homes or hospitals because their birth parents cannot or will not care for them. The children receive adequate medical care, but overburdened nurses and other staff are not able to provide the personal nurturing that young children need. Because of the sterile, restrictive hospital setting, youngsters may develop psychological problems, some so severe that the children fail to thrive physically.

As an alternative to long-term hospitalization, the Children's Crisis Center of Jacksonville, Florida, set up a Medical Foster Care program. Through the program, begun in 1980, registered nurses are recruited for short-term foster parenting. These foster parents are of course licensed to practice nursing and also, after intensive training, are able to teach birth parents the skills needed to care for their children. Along with providing treatment for complex medical problems, the main goal is to help the biological family function in constructive ways and to maintain and improve the bond between birth parents and their children.

Another type of foster care program for hospitalized children is in effect in a number of big-city hospitals. The program serves so-called boarder babies whose parents have abandoned them or are unable to care for them, so they have given up custody. Volunteers act as foster parents (or grandparents) for an hour or two per week, giving their time to hold, cuddle, and rock infants who wait in hospital wards for foster or adoptive homes. If the babies are healthy, they may be placed in foster care or adoptive homes in a few days. But those with special needs may wait months or years for homes. After eight months, hospitals usually place special needs children in nursing homes or other institutions. Unfortunately, many of the babies have multiple handicaps, and an increasing number are born with AIDS.

Although some foster and adoptive parents are willing to take babies born with AIDS, most refuse because they fear being infected with the virus. However, medical experts assure prospective foster parents that AIDS is not transmitted by casual contact. Rather, the virus is spread by intimate sexual contact, by transfusions of blood tainted with the virus, by drug abusers who share contaminated needles, and by mothers with AIDS who pass the disease to their children before or at birth.

One of the most painful aspects of caring for AIDS babies is coping with the emotional strain of knowing that they may not live more than two years or at the most up to six years. This can be devastating. But as one foster mother said: "I try to provide the children with as much love as possible during the time they have, and do the best I can for them, one day at a time."

Whatever the special needs of some children, it is clear that they are not considered "burdens" to their adoptive and foster parents or other caregivers. On the contrary, many a foster or adoptive parent has been quick to describe the joy and love they share with their children.

In her book *Beating the Adoption Game*, author Cynthia Martin summed up a chapter on special children, pointing out that they are categorized under "special needs" in order to "discuss them separately. . . .Their specialness is a label for our convenience in considering them. On a personal basis . . . they are specific people with unique sets of needs, desires, hopes, and dreams. . . .Ultimately, no one has such a handle on life that in some way he or she could not be labeled a 'special needs person.' "

8

"Mixed" Foster and Adoptive Families

The United States is not a melting pot. It has never been, and it's not going to be. I believe Jewish kids should be raised by Jewish parents, Indian kids should be raised by Indian parents, and so forth.

> —*a policy statement of the National Association of Black Social Workers*

You're asking them [black children] to move into a family and build a parent-child relationship, and take it on as their own family. That is difficult enough without them moving into a white culture.

> —*a supervisor in New York's Department of Human Services, as quoted in The New York Times*

Even though it's a violation of our U.S. Constitution and the 1964 U.S. Civil Rights Act, we still have agencies who don't recruit minority families for minority children, but hold them in foster care while turning away different-race families who could meet a child's needs. We still have workers who rigidly insist on like-race placements or nothing.

—*president of the National Coalition to End Racism in America's Child Care System*

These arguments really come down to a basic question: Is it in the best interests of children to place them with foster or adoptive families who are not of the same racial or religious background? Some child care workers would respond with a flat "No." Others say that matching by race or religion should be only one criterion in determining the placement of foster or adoptive children who wait for homes.

Although there is a great debate over cross-racial/cultural adoptions, Bart and Nancy Lefever adopted Jed and Courtney. They moved from an all-white neighborhood to a "mixed" neighborhood as a means of helping their children identify with and maintain ties with their African-American heritage.

Why the Debate?

Throughout the nation's history, most people have formed families that reflected the racial, religious, or ethnic group into which they were born. (An ethnic group usually shares a national heritage and culture, or way of life.) People also tended to form families within the same social or economic groups. Couples who formed families outside their particular groups were considered "unnatural" because of the dominant view that people should "stick with their own kind or class."

Actually, a great number of Americans still believe that racial, religious, or ethnic mixing in families is "wrong," "abnormal," or at best "peculiar." Others take a broader view, realizing that people share many commonalities, even though in a pluralistic society individuals may differ from one another in appearance, native language, or religious belief.

During the 1950s and 1960s, there was a decline in the number of white Anglo Saxon babies—babies whose birth parents were of northern European heritage—available for adoption. Thus, white couples sought children of other racial or ethnic groups. But adoption agencies in the United States and Canada were originally set up to serve Anglo (white) families—to place healthy white infants with childless couples. Older white children, handicapped youngsters, and children of color (minorities) were considered "hard to place" or "unadoptable." In fact, there were few services for minority children in the child care system or for prospective adopters.

Only as it became clear that the number of minority children in need of services was increasing did agencies begin to see that they had to find adoptive families for them. One of the first agencies to address this need was the Open Door Society of Montreal, Canada. Later, the Council on Adoptable Children was set up in the United States, and a variety of other groups were established in North America and Europe to promote adoption of minority youngsters.

At the same time that U.S. public and private social service agencies began to place a fairly large number of American minority children with white families, white couples also were adopting children from other countries. Intercountry adoptions began in the United States as a way to help European children who were orphaned during World War II. But in recent years, because of lower birthrates, very few white European children have been available for adoption. Of the nearly 10,000 foreign adoptions each year in the United States, most of the children come from Asian and Latin American countries.

Ironically, placing foreign-born children, who are classified in the United States as minorities, with white American families seems to be more acceptable in U.S. society than similar placements of American-born minority children. In the early 1970s, more than 2,000 minority children were placed with white families each year, but that number has dropped significantly, according to federal reports. As one U.S. adoptive family noted: "It's easier for a white family to adopt a dark-skinned foreign child than to adopt a U.S. child who is labeled 'black,' 'Indian,' 'Hispanic,' or some other color-coded term."

The decrease in mixed foster and adoptive families is directly related to the rise in racial pride that followed the civil rights movement of the 1960s. African-American and Native American groups especially have increased their efforts to match foster and adoptive children with families who share their particular heritages. For example, since 1972, the National Association of Black Social Workers has been publicly opposed to placing black children in white homes. The organization claims such a placement would destroy the children's racial identity, and black children raised in white homes would not learn the coping skills needed to deal with white society's long-held negative view of blacks. The group argues as well that when black children are raised in a black community, they have the support of other blacks who have had to learn appropriate ways to handle white actions and attitudes that attempt to demean black people.

In other arguments, black professionals point out that the vast majority of social workers are white and know little about black culture. Thus they have judged black families by white styles of parenting and middle-class living standards. Since many black families live in neighborhoods that whites have labeled "undesirable," white social workers, it is believed, also view black families as "undesirable" adopters.

Recruiting Homes for Black Children

Because of white dominance of the child welfare system, there has been little effort, until recently, to actively recruit black adoptive families. As a result, a number of state child welfare departments have been sponsoring media campaigns—using posters, flyers, brochures, and TV and radio announcements—to inform black families about the need for adoptive homes for black children.

Other efforts in the past few years include those of predominantly black organizations such as Homes for Black Children founded in Detroit and One Church, One Child first established in Chicago. The goal of the One Church, One Child program, which has chapters throughout the United States, is to recruit from each black church one black family to adopt a black child. In many black communities, the majority of families are involved with local black churches, so the program can reach a large number of potential adopters.

Church families may look through adoption books with pictures and background information about children who wait for permanent homes, and may take on the responsibility of finding an adoptive family for a child. According to the director of the Indiana One Church, One Child program, the children who need homes are "typically eight years old or older and may be members of foster homes or challenged by physical or mental problems. If the children are not placed in permanent homes, they risk developing mental disorders."

Laws Regarding Indian Adoptees

Racial matching is also a concern of Indian tribes. Representatives of some Indian tribes, church groups, and state and federal legislators have supported laws that require adoption agencies to make special efforts to place Indian children with Indian families. The federal

Indian Child Welfare Act (ICWA), for example, gives tribal courts the right to determine with whom Indian children will be placed, whether for foster care or for adoption. Even Indian mothers who place their children for adoption and Indian children who do not live on reservations come under the range of the law.

ICWA was designed to correct past child welfare practices that discriminated against Indian children on reservations. For many years, white social workers and others working with Indian families have reported them to be "dysfunctional"—unable to care for the needs of their children. The judgment was often based on the poverty of the family, not necessarily on how it functioned. Children might be removed from a home just because there was no indoor bathroom or because the home was considered "too small" for the size of the family.

Indian groups also have charged that social workers seldom tried to place Indian children with their relatives or with other tribal families. Social workers ignored or knew little about the importance of the extended family (which includes members of the tribal community) in Indian culture. As one researcher has pointed out:

> The dynamics of Native-American extended families . . . are little understood by outsiders. A Native American may have scores or perhaps more than a hundred relatives who are counted as close, responsible members of the family. Many outsiders, untutored in the ways of Native-American life, assume only the parents to be responsible, and interpret the acceptance of responsibility for a child by persons outside of the nuclear family as neglect or abuse.

The Debate Goes On

The importance of recognizing and being sensitive to the heritage of adoptees has been reflected in child welfare policies established over the past decade. Some child welfare agencies emphasize that vigorous efforts *should* be made to place a foster or adoptive child with adoptees who are similar in background to the child's birth family. But such policies frequently have been interpreted to mean that placement of nonwhites with whites must be ruled out *entirely*. As one social worker in Buffalo, New York, said: "It is the height of racism to assume that black people cannot take care of their own!"

Yet no such racist assumption is made by the majority of people who adopt a child whose color is different from their own. As studies have shown, people adopt across color lines for the very same reasons that people make like-race adoptions: they want a child to love and care for.

Because of the emphasis during the past decade on matching children to families by race, hundreds of children have been denied the opportunity to be part of a foster or adoptive family. In addition, many foster children have been removed from homes where they have lived for many months and even years in order to better color-match them with other families.

One Detroit case, which was reported in newspapers nationwide during the mid-1980s, involved a white couple, Karen and Guenther Lahr, who wanted to adopt Deanna, an infant biracial girl. One of Deanna's birth parents was white, the other black. But as often is the case the child was labeled black, even though she was also biologically part white.

Deanna was placed with the Lahrs at the age of one month. A Down syndrome (mentally retarded) child with a severe heart problem, Deanna was so weak on her arrival that she could hardly cry. She developed pneumonia and came close to death, but with medical help the Lahrs nursed her back to health. Then two months before her first birthday Deanna underwent surgery to correct her failing heart.

With all the medical problems and caring for Deanna, the Lahrs soon bonded with the child and a month after surgery decided to apply to adopt her. They believed they were well prepared to raise Deanna since they had successfully raised two birth children to adulthood and had been foster parents over the years for thirty-six children. Most of the foster children were members of minority groups; some had physical or mental disabilities.

But the Lahr's application was turned down. A social worker informed them that the policy of the child welfare service was to first consider a black couple as adoptive parents. If no black couple could be found, then a white couple might be considered. A little over a year after Deanna had been placed with the Lahrs, the social worker informed them that Deanna would be placed with a black adoptive family. However, at the Lahrs' request, the American Civil Liberties Union took the case to court, and a restraining order was granted. At the hearing, the circuit court judge ruled that an independent adoption agency would make the decision about who would adopt Deanna.

Several months later, the agency director recommended that the Lahrs be granted their request to adopt. In her letter to the Lahrs, the agency director wrote: "It appears that Deanna already regards you as her parents. That fact, coupled with her age, the length of time she has

Molly, who is part of a large family of adopted and birth children, enjoys the use of a home computer.

lived with you, your demonstrated ability to meet her special physical needs, and her current stage of development, lead me to conclude that it could not be in her best interests to move her to a new home at this time."

After hearing about this and similar cases, one Detroit man pointed out some absurdities involved in trying to color-match families:

> I am white and my wife is black. . . .My daughter, being a biracial child, carries the heritage of two great people. She is neither white nor black, but both. . . .The black social workers' group says that biracial children are better accepted and more comfortable in black communities because of the history of racism in this country. Well, I certainly don't dispute our country's racist history, nor do I maintain that there is no more racism in America. But . . . there are enough racists for every group to have its share. My daughter is hated by some for being too white just as she is for being too black. . . .The irony is that because my family would be classified as a white family . . . we couldn't adopt our own child if my wife hadn't borne her.

Attempts to Resolve Conflicts

According to the Civil Rights Office of the U.S. Department of Human Services, child welfare agencies receiving federal funds "are in violation of Title VI if they categorically prohibit adoptions or foster care placement on the basis of race, color, or national origin." At the forefront of efforts to prevent such violations is the National Coalition to End Racism in America's Child Care System (NCERACCS), under the direction of Carol Coccia of Taylor, Michigan. Carol and her husband, Dan, who heads the Michigan Foster Parents Association, have been foster parents for more than twenty years. They have personally "known the damage children suffer" when moved to another home only for the purpose of color matching. As Carol noted: "According to therapists, some of my foster children will have lifelong problems in their ability to attach or maintain relationships; the damage will be present through adulthood and will probably require years of therapy."

Frank Ehlers, a Michigan social worker and editor of the NCERACCS newsletter, has noted that the debate over matching children by race has made children pawns in political power struggles. In a brief article for the newsletter, Ehlers provided an example of this conflict, which he had observed while attending a national conference on foster and adoptive care:

> In a workshop conducted by Native-American social workers, the speaker said that if a child has one African-American parent and one Native-American parent, that child must be placed in a Native-American family or one approved by the Tribal Council. Upon the conclusion of that workshop, I attended one conducted by African-American social workers. During that workshop the speaker said that if a child has one Native-American parent and one African-American parent, that child must be placed in an African-American family.

Resolving these conflicting positions requires that people "stop thinking and acting in a racist manner," Ehlers wrote. "Just place the child with a loving and caring family that acknowledges, accepts and appreciates *all* of the child's racial and cultural heritage and teaches the child to do the same."

Sydney Duncan, director of the Detroit Homes for Black Children, also has spoken out on this issue. In a speech before a group of adoption and foster care workers, she explained the turmoil that she and others like her have experienced:

> For those of us who are black the pain has been the fear of losing our destiny through the loss of our children. For those of you who are white and have adopted [across color lines] the pain has been the denial of your right to parent a child. . . .For [the children] it is the pain of being caught in the middle of the struggle. Any time adults argue about children, it has to threaten the security of children. And if someone is arguing about the rightness of your home, that is the ultimate threat. It is the threat of the loss of your home. It does not allow you to settle in and become secure.

Duncan called for people within the child care system to put differences aside and to begin to work for understanding. She also expressed the hope that workers would be flexible and would consider individual foster or adoptive family situations when determining where children should be placed.

Perhaps the point is best made by a woman who, as a child, lived in ten different foster homes and two children's homes before she was adopted at the age of twelve. The only reason she was not placed earlier was she was labeled a minority child. In this women's view, any refusal to provide a permanent home to a child solely because of a racial, religious, or an ethnic difference between the child and prospective parents is "a blatant hostile act against the best interest of the child."

9

Crises in the Child Care System

How can the child welfare system be made to work in the best interests of children? That was one of the major questions posed during congressional hearings held in Washington, D.C. A congressional committee called the hearings in 1988 as part of its review of the Adoption Assistance and Child Welfare Act. Passed in 1980, the act was designed to encourage adoption of special needs children and to stop the shuffling of young people from one foster home to another.

The law provides federal subsidies to help families pay for medical, therapeutic, and other services. In addition, the act provides funds for state child welfare programs that are supposed to provide various family services such as counseling and homemaking aid. These services can help families function more effectively and can help reunite foster children with their birth families. If children who are wards of the court cannot be reunited with their families of origin, the federal law mandates that within eighteen months the children must be placed in a long-term foster home or an adoptive home.

Basic Problems in the System

Witnesses who testified before the congressional committee charged that federal and state governments are not enforcing the law. Also, because of funding cuts, there are not enough caseworkers and other personnel to provide the services needed for the increasing number of children in foster care. One New York child welfare supervisor testified that each city caseworker handles well over forty cases, twice the professional standard of twenty to twenty-five per caseworker. "New York City's child protective services system is in crisis," the supervisor said. "It is severely overburdened and understaffed."

A number of newspaper and national magazine features have underscored the crisis situation in New York's child care system. An investigative report in the *Daily News*, for example, revealed that babies and young children who have been neglected or abused are being placed in substandard city-run group homes to wait for placement with foster families, which are in short supply. According to the report, the city's health department "began inspecting the group homes after the deaths . . . of two children who lived in a home run by a private agency in Brooklyn." During a six-month inspection period, the department found many health and safety violations and overcrowding.

The New York Times reported in late 1988 that a study, ordered by a federal district judge, revealed "a deeply troubled foster care system [that] has temporarily kept hundreds of children in violence-plagued, cramped and poorly equipped field offices." Children who are in custody of the city's child welfare agency are brought to the various field offices to await placement. But because of the shortage of foster homes, the children may be shuffled to an emergency home for the night and then be back in the field offices the next day.

The *Times* pointed out, however, that the court-ordered study of the foster care system "was not entirely critical." For example, one section of the report noted that a majority of the child welfare workers were dedicated and sensitive to children's needs. They were often frustrated by the poor conditions in the field offices. Workers also were upset about the detailed paperwork required and by what they saw as "lack of support from the city."

Similar complaints are aired in other cities across the nation. Overcrowding and staff shortages in child protective agencies lead to scandals, such as the rape of an eight-year-old boy staying in an emergency service center operated by Chicago's Department of Children and Family Services. According to a *Chicago Tribune* report, two twelve-year-old boys, also in custody at the emergency center, "forced the younger boy to engage in various sex acts."

At the time the assault took place, nearly fifty boys and girls were staying overnight in the shelter, waiting for placement in other facilities or foster homes. There were only four child care workers in the shelter that night even though the center's license "calls for one worker for every five children." According to one staff person, the facility had many "nooks and crannies" and was so overcrowded that it was impossible to monitor.

Other, more gruesome and tragic cases of children being harmed because of their placements in the child care system were described in a *Christian Science Monitor* report—the result of a six-month investigation of children in state custody. The report mentioned the following cases:

- a San Francisco foster child who was bludgeoned to death

- two foster children in Boston who were poisoned

- a Philadelphia child who was literally shaken to death while in foster care

- foster children in New Orleans who were sexually abused by foster parents

How can such tragedies occur? Why are children who are wards of the state placed in abusive foster homes? Where are the workers who are supposed to monitor foster homes and the welfare of foster children?

Causes of the Child Care Crisis

Many argue that along with overburdened facilities and staff shortages, the problem of the high turnover rate of child care workers contributes to the chaos in the child welfare system. As a Maine foster mother reported: ''My husband and I have been foster parents for over ten years and we have cared for seventeen children in our home. With each new child came a different social worker and a new relationship.''

Problems in the child care system are compounded by the fact that some child care workers have little understanding of how to handle emotionally disturbed children or troubled teenagers with drug and other behavior problems. The same can be said for some foster and adoptive parents—they may be overwhelmed by children with multiple problems. Without help from agencies to obtain therapy for children, legal or medical aid, or special education, a foster care or adoptive placement can break down, or disrupt, as agencies call it.

An example is a foster/adoptive family in West Seneca, New York, who asked their agency to remove a six-year-old foster child from their home. "The boy's behavior and response to authority were so poor that normal family activities had to be curtailed," the foster mother explained. She added that the child welfare agency "withheld important information about the boy and thwarted efforts to get counseling for him." As a result, the foster mother said she would foster only infants from now on and was "afraid to try again" with children any older.

Several studies during the past decade showed that most disruptions in adoptions involve so-called high-risk children—older children, children with multiple problems, and children who had been sexually abused. However, various characteristics of adoptive families also contributed to the disruptions. As one study pointed out: "Traditional middle-class families may expect the child to conform in ways not possible. One mother became disgruntled because the child absolutely refused to have a normal breakfast and make his bed each morning. Another consistently would not feed the family dog. Over time these transgressions of family 'rules' became bones of contention described as major contributing factors to the disruption."

On the positive side, the same studies that attempt to find the causes of disruptions in adoption also show that the majority of adoptive families with "high-risk kids" are stable. Disruptions are not as likely to occur if parents have received adequate information about the special needs of their children. Subsidies to help pay the costs of medical care and therapy and moral support from extended family members and other adoptive parents also seemed to be important factors in successful adoptions.

Need for Social Services

Many child care experts point out that a variety of social services are needed to keep not only adoptive families but also foster and birth families together. The crisis situation in the nation's child care system has its roots, many believe, in the tremendous cuts in federal social programs that were designed to help families meet basic human needs. Reports from various national organizations show that in spite of the nation's economic growth over the past two decades, the number of people living in poverty has increased by at least seven million since 1980.

The largest group of poor in the United States are children. In fact, "The rate of child poverty in the United States is 60 percent higher than it is in Great Britain and more than double the rate in West Germany, Norway and Sweden," according to a report by the League of Women Voters Education Fund. The report noted that while social programs in the United States were being cut during the 1980s, "Many western European nations were increasing assistance to their populations—especially families and children. These countries now provide a variety of income supplements—family allowances, housing assistance and government-generated child support—to buttress widely available job training, child care and health care programs."

Although unemployment rates in the United States are low, "most of the 16 million new jobs that have been created since 1980 are service-sector jobs," noted *U.S. News & World Report*. Many of these jobs pay the minimum wage or slightly more—well below the amount needed to provide for the basic needs of a family of four.

Poverty in turn is linked to family violence, homelessness, lack of education and job skills, poor nutrition and health, and death. An estimated 10,000 children die each year because of poverty-related problems. Malnutrition, for example, leads to infant mortality and such health problems as anemia and mental retardation.

Hunger and malnutrition are widespread among the poor. The U.S. Conference of Mayors reported that in recent years requests for emergency food assistance in major cities had increased sharply. Many of the rural poor, who total 9.7 million, also suffer from life-threatening illnesses or health problems brought on by malnutrition.

The lack of affordable housing is having an impact on millions of poor families, who must spend well over half of their income for rent. Unemployment, divorce, serious illness, or other catastrophe combines with the continual rise in the cost of housing to put poor families out on the street. An estimated 40 percent of the three to four million homeless in the United States are families with children who may find refuge for a time in a crowded shelter or abandoned building. Some live in cars or stay overnight in parks or public facilities such as train stations. Homelessness often results in abuse and neglect of children and certainly has an effect on children's education and health.

The high cost of health care is one more major problem that contributes to the child welfare crisis. Few people in jobs paying the minimum wage receive benefits such as paid or partly paid health insurance premiums. As a result, low-income families seldom are able to afford health care, particularly for members with severe and chronic physical or emotional problems—a situation that can prompt parents to place special needs children in the custody of child welfare agencies.

Although emergency medical care may be available for some, preventive care is another matter. Through various public and private programs, some low-income families receive prenatal care, nutrition information, immunizations for childhood diseases, and similar services. But many other health care services that could prevent illnesses—counseling for alcoholism and drug addiction, therapy for the abused, and sex education—are not within the reach of the majority of poor families. Once again, not meeting such needs adds to the overload on the child care system.

Another national crisis—the shortage of day care facilities—contributes to the number of children who become wards of the court. Well over half of the preschool children in the nation have moms who work outside the home. Many of these mothers are single women, earning low wages. Even if day care for their children is available, single mothers cannot afford the cost and while on the job may leave their children unattended or with unreliable baby sitters. If

This family, who live in a homeless shelter, have little to do except watch television.

they are not properly supervised, the children may become victims of household fires, poisoning, or other hazards. Parents may then be charged with neglect.

Louis Harris, a well-known pollster, has noted that a majority of Americans want "government to provide day-care services for children of poor working mothers." At least 90 percent of those polled believe the federal government should be providing health insurance for children and families who cannot afford it.

Other major polls have indicated that a growing number of Americans also favor spending government funds—and would agree to tax increases to do so—for family services. These would include prenatal care for poor mothers, immunizations for children, job training, and birth control services for teenagers. As Harris observed, "It is obvious . . . that the American people have come to a new consciousness about children. . . . The public is ready for leadership to emerge that will call upon them to make those sacrifices necessary for government and the private sector to take action in behalf of children."

10

Supporting and Preserving Families

Action in behalf of children takes many forms. It might be medical aid or a school lunch program or day care. Or it might be an educational program such as the highly successful and federally funded Head Start program. Established in the 1960s, the program involves parents and young children from low-income families. It provides information and help in basic educational skills that give youngsters a head start on formal schooling.

Other actions that benefit children include setting up support programs to preserve and strengthen families. Some of these programs help parents reduce stress and learn to cope. Support programs have been developing on a wide scale over the past two or three decades, but the idea of providing support for families is not new. Since the early days of the nation, rural families could count on the support of others in their community.

Even though a farm family might be primarily self-sufficient—providing their own food, clothing, housing, health care, education, and so on—the family received help building a barn or bringing in the harvest. Neighbors stepped in to provide the extra labor.

Women shared work in the fields and information on child care. They got together to help each other quilt or to cook during harvests. People rallied around to be of service when a family member became seriously ill or died. Farm communities also came together to celebrate marriages and holidays. This type of mutual support is still evident in some rural areas.

Social Changes That Have Affected Families

As families moved to cities, they seldom had a network of supportive people to turn to for advice, information, or material aid. With the expansion of industry and business, more and more diverse people came to live and work in urban areas. There was an increasing need for support groups and organizations to provide the services that had been common in small rural communities.

For example, programs that provide prenatal and infant care and nursing and medical services for older family members have been around for nearly a century. Organizations such as the Parent-Teacher Association (PTA) have long helped educate families on child development and child-rearing practices. Alcoholics Anonymous, which provides moral support and techniques to deal with health and behavior problems, is just one of many self-help programs that have a long history. Early settlement houses—the famous Hull House established by Jane Addams in Chicago is an example—were established in urban communities during the late 1800s and early 1900s to help poor immigrant families take action to better their lives.

Today's numerous and varied family support programs have their roots in the settlement house movement, according to Bernice Weissbourd, who heads the Family Resource Coalition, a national network of family support programs. "Many of today's parents are immigrants of a different kind, the newly mobile population that stays in the same place for a short time before moving on," Weissbourd wrote. She noted that, like immigrants in a new country, many families today often feel uprooted. They do not have an extended family (grandparents, aunts, uncles, and so on) nearby to provide emotional support or material help, and seldom do they have the information and resources to make changes to improve their environment and family life.

Mobility is not the only factor that contributes to family change and the need for support programs. As has frequently been pointed out in news stories and studies, there were profound changes in family structures during the 1980s. About half of all marriages will end in divorce, if current rates continue, which means that one out of four children can be expected to live in a single-parent home. But most divorced adults remarry and in many instances will add to the increasing number of "blended" families, or stepfamilies.

These changes in family forms have set the stage for the establishment of national support groups such as Parents Without Partners and the Step Family Foundation. Local programs include the New York Sisterhood of Black Single Mothers and groups formed by divorced fathers.

Along with family structural changes, a vast number of people have experienced role changes. No longer, as was the case in the 1950s, do the majority of women work only in the home while men work at jobs outside the home. Today women make up nearly half of the total labor force in the United States, and by the year 2000 at least three out of five new workers are expected to be women. Yet even in households where both the woman and the man work outside the home, the woman still handles most household chores and child care duties, creating stress not only for the woman but for the family as well. To deal with stressful situations, there are such support services as day care, infant care, teenage and other parenting programs, child abuse programs, and shelters for battered women and children.

Although women are increasingly self-sufficient, a growing number of women have little chance to earn high incomes. According to an economist at the Economic Policy Institute, the average income of families headed by divorced or single mothers is 55 percent less than that of households headed by unmarried men. It is 50 percent less than that of families in which the woman stays home. This has been brought about in part because many divorced women and young single mothers have few or no job skills. A large number of support programs have been set up to help women learn new skills or to obtain a college degree.

Dealing With Child Abuse

Support programs also help families with severe health problems, drug addiction, alcoholism, emotional illness, mental disabilities, or other difficulties that can lead to neglect and abuse of children. Reports of these problems have increased dramatically since 1976 because of widespread public education on symptoms of maltreatment. Also, laws require that social workers, teachers, medical personnel, and other professionals dealing with children report suspected abuse.

Although some reported cases are not valid, 53 percent are confirmed instances of abuse or neglect. This is considered a high percentage when compared to other types of emergency calls, such as reporting a fire—nationwide, only a third involve an actual fire. Yet child care experts believe that thousands of cases of child abuse are not reported. Perhaps as many as 5,000 children died of abuse in one year alone—1987—rather than the 1,200 fatalities actually reported and linked to abuse.

According to Deborah Daro, director of the National Center on Child Abuse Prevention Research, many cases may be dismissed because there appears to be no outward sign of brutality, sexual abuse, or severe neglect—but "Child maltreatment encompasses a range of parental behaviors, some of which . . . have less visible but potentially very damaging, impacts. . . .Reports involving apparent minor physical mistreatment or failure to provide adequate care can and do escalate with serious, even fatal, consequences for children."

One widely publicized case was that of six-year-old Lisa Steinberg. Joel Steinberg, a new York attorney, and Hedda Nussbaum, a former children's book editor, were raising Lisa as an adopted daughter. Lisa's birth mother had left her child with Joel Steinberg and had paid him a $500 fee to place Lisa with an adoptive family. Instead, Steinberg kept the child but never legally adopted her. For most of Lisa's short life he would regularly beat and abuse her. Steinberg also physically and psychologically abused Nussbaum, who was so battered and beaten that she could not come to Lisa's defense. Steinberg's violence eventually caused Lisa's death.

In January 1989 Joel Steinberg was convicted of first-degree manslaughter. During the sentencing, the judge recommended that Steinberg be denied parole since he showed no remorse or accepted no responsibility for his crime. Because of the Steinberg case the state of New York passed a law that requires teachers and school administrators to be trained in the symptoms of child abuse and how to take action against it.

There have been a number of extreme and controversial methods suggested for dealing with abusive parents. During the summer of 1988, an Indiana Superior Court judge, for example, wanted to order sterilization for a mother who had killed her four-year-old son by poisoning. The judge said he believed the woman, who was pregnant again and had attempted suicide, had "no need for any more children." But an American Civil Liberties Union (ACLU) lawyer said the judge's punishment, if allowed, would be "outrageous" and that the woman needed psychiatric help.

In another case that same summer, an Arizona judge ordered a similar punishment for a woman who had left her two infant sons alone for three days. The woman was required to use birth control until she was no longer able to bear children. Again, however, the ACLU stepped in, saying the order violated the woman's reproductive rights. The Catholic church also objected on the grounds that the woman's religious beliefs would be violated if she used birth control.

Another suggestion came from one American and three Czech researchers who studied what they termed "unwanted" children. Their study concluded that pregnant women who do not want to bear children should be encouraged to obtain an abortion. According to the researchers, if women give birth to unwanted children, they may abuse them. Unwanted children also are more likely to suffer emotional problems or engage in criminal behavior than other children.

However, sterilization, birth control, and abortion are not widely accepted in the United States as methods for dealing with abuse and neglect. Instead, programs and policies to protect children from mistreatment are geared toward preserving families if at all possible and intervening to protect children when necessary.

Home Based Services

According to the U.S. Department of Health and Human Services, one of the most rapidly growing areas of child welfare is providing home-based services that will help families deal with crisis situations and prevent removal of children from their families of origin. Home-based or family-based programs vary from state to state and agency to agency. But the services provided generally include treatment for alcohol and drug abuse, crisis intervention, legal and medical aid, family therapy, and education in child development and parenting skills.

Family-based services have come about in part because of a change in emphasis in social work. The idea of "rescuing" a child from his or her family has been replaced with the concept of preserving birth families. In addition, the Indian Child Welfare Act of 1978 and the Child Welfare Act of 1980 require that child welfare agencies make "reasonable efforts" to provide services that will keep families intact.

The main purpose of both federal statutes is to use foster care placement only when it is absolutely necessary to protect the health and safety of children. Judges who make the decisions on whether children should be in protective custody must first determine that child welfare agencies have complied with federal laws.

To meet the legal requirements, child welfare workers must make a thorough evaluation of families and provide services that will eliminate or reduce risks to children. At the same time, workers cannot be too intrusive on families. Services also must be sensitive to and respect racial/cultural differences in families.

Home-based services have proven effective with many minority families. As Kenton Williams, a human development specialist in a regional Health and Human Services office in Boston, wrote:

> Minorities, particularly blacks, feel isolated from the mainstream of society, and to venture from their homes and neighborhoods is to enter a strange and hostile world. When a family support program is located in the neighborhood or black community, the agency becomes a part of the community and relieves the disquiet some family members feel when they leave their familiar surroundings. . . .Institutions in the black community, such as the church, fraternal orders, civil rights organizations, and social clubs, play an important role in family life and are critical to any family support effort. These organizations are paying increased attention to the plight of the black family and the undermining forces of drugs, crime, unemployment, poor health, and teenage pregnancy.

Of the many types of family- or home-based services offered, intensive crisis counseling is one of the most effective in preserving any "at-risk" family, no matter what the racial/cultural background. Modeled after a Washington State program called Homebuilders, crisis counseling has become part of several state child welfare programs. Families referred for counseling usually have multiple problems, including unemployment, children with severe emotional disturbances, and other difficult situations that lead to stress and then abuse.

Counselors may visit a family several times a week to help a parent get financial assistance, work with schools to assist their children with problems, and deal with child care and home management. Child welfare workers say that crisis counseling has helped reduce violence in the home and thus has reduced the number of children who have to be removed from their birth homes and placed in foster care.

Another example of how home-based services work is a program called Supportive Child Adult Network (SCAN), which began in Philadelphia and now is a model for other urban areas. SCAN serves families that have a history of child abuse and neglect. In Philadelphia, most of the SCAN families are headed by single parents who are eighteen years old or younger and are receiving some type of welfare payments. As a report on the program noted:

> Many of the families live in substandard apartments or public housing projects that are overcrowded, unsanitary and often have neither heat nor other uilities. Many lack adequate food . . . almost 50 percent of the parents suffer significant depression; 50 percent have alcohol or drug related problems; and 25 percent function at a low intellectual level. Some of the parents have never learned to love or are unaware of children's needs and the stages of child development; some are unable to accept the total dependency of a young child.

To help such families function and to prevent possible abuse and separation of children from their parents, social workers, counselors, and other caregivers teach effective parenting and communication, money management, decision making, and conflict resolution. SCAN staff often share child care tasks. A worker, for example, might feed a child or model appropriate behavior for disciplining a child without harsh treatment. Perhaps a worker will go with a parent on a shopping trip to explain how to check prices and get the best buys in food or other necessities. In addition, staff members provide home nursing, which includes nutrition information. They also help families contact community agencies that can provide legal aid, emergency housing, or other services when needed.

How Foster Care Helps Reunite Families

Although there are successful programs to prevent unnecessary placement of children in foster care, thousands of children and youth still become part of the system each year. As previously noted, the increase in social and economic problems—from drug abuse to poverty—and crises in the child welfare system contribute to foster care placements. But there are also efforts underway to help children reunite with their families of origin.

Many of those efforts involve foster parents who have been trained to work with and act as a resource for birth parents. This is not an easy task since foster parents and birth parents can easily be in conflict.

Birth parents may feel they have been unfairly treated. Foster parents might resent birth parents whose actions have resulted in a child's placement in foster care. There could be competition between foster parents and birth parents for a child's affection and loyalty. Any number of other reasons can create conflict and antagonism between foster and birth parents. However, foster parents who see themselves as "professional parents," and receive training and support from child welfare agencies, usually can nurture the child and also help a family reunite.

Community sports programs help to maintain family relationships. Here a foster father works with his foster son and others in a boxing program.

In order to reunite families, foster children have to maintain their relationship with their birth parents through planned visitation. Courts and child welfare agency policies determine how often and where visits will take place. Depending on the circumstances surrounding the placement, foster children might visit with their birth parents for a few hours or a weekend in their own home, or for a fixed time in the foster home or in an agency office. The court can deny visitation if a birth parent endangers or threatens the life of a child or if there are severe problems while visiting.

Visitations can be trying and frustrating for all involved—children, caseworkers, foster and birth parents. During training sessions, most foster parents learn about difficulties children, particularly young children, face when they visit. For example, young children may not understand what is happening to them and may react to a visit by withdrawing, by crying, or by becoming belligerent.

Most foster children want to be with their birth parents. Even though birth parents may not be ideal, they are Mom and Dad. A foster child's feelings of frustration and rejection are brought to the surface during a visit.

Foster parents also may have to deal with the disappointments of children whose birth parents have made promises they cannot fulfill. "It's like the kid visits in a fairyland," one foster mother said. "The birth mother brings gifts, tells her child things are going to be just great, but there is no money, no home, no resources. I really can't blame the mom—she wants her child back. But the child can't understand why things aren't working out as Mom promised."

While helping families reunite, foster parents may serve as models for birth parents. For example, one foster mother bought a cake mix and helped a birth mother to bake the cake for her son's birthday. Another foster parent encouraged an exchange of letters between a foster child and her birth mother, who was in prison. In another instance, a foster father invited a biological father to join in various family activities—a picnic, an evening of bowling, a trip to the zoo—to encourage him to relate to his child in a personal way.

Getting involved with and setting examples for birth parents are very much a part of foster care in a program set up by the Center for Family Life in Brooklyn. This Catholic agency, operated by two nuns, is committed to keeping families together. To do so, the nuns place children in foster homes within the neighborhood where the birth parents live. As Sister Mary Paul told a *Daily News* reporter: "It's traumatic enough for children to be separated from their parents at an early age, but we also feel it's damaging to leave their friends and everything familiar." The nuns encourage birth parents, some of whom are young teenagers, to visit their children in the foster homes. They also train foster parents to help birth parents learn child care

Carole Lukacek reads a letter from a former foster son who describes how much he appreciated living with the Lukacek family. Carole and her husband Michael have been foster parents for many years and have provided emergency foster care for hundreds of children and young people in Illinois.

techniques, the preparation of nutritious foods, positive ways to discipline, and other parenting skills.

Whatever methods are used to get families back together or keep them intact, there is little doubt that the process can be difficult. Someimes it is impossible if birth parents cannot be rehabilitated to provide a safe and healthy environment for their children. When children cannot return to their birth parents, child care experts say every effort should be made to terminate parental rights as soon as possible, so that children are not "in limbo," being shuffled from place to place. The point is to get children into permanent homes today, not years from now.

11

People Who Protect Children

- A doctor in a mobile medical van makes a stop to treat children at a shabby New York City hotel that is a temporary shelter for homeless families.

- A volunteer answers one of many hundreds of emergency calls coming in each year to an Illinois hotline for kids suffering abuse.

- A worker in a California crisis center counsels a single mother under severe stress who fears she will abuse her infant son.

- A caseworker in Florida visits a desperate family and helps them get food stamps, day care for two young children, and rental assistance.

- A foster parent in New Mexico attends a training class on dealing with the behavior problems of children who have long been in foster care.

- A counselor in Pennsylvania conducts a therapy session with the intent of helping parents reunite with their children who are in a group home.

- A teacher in Utah teaches homeless children in a "School With No Name," a metal shack near a track where converted railroad cars shelter seventy-five to one hundred residents.

These people are examples of "front-line" workers who try to protect children and preserve families. Another example is a juvenile court judge. Usually a judge is seen as one who punishes rather than one who protects. But a juvenile court judge is responsible for making decisions that sometimes save lives, particularly if those decisions remove children from severely abusive or dangerously neglectful homes. For example, a judge might have to make such a decision in regard to a baby born addicted to cocaine or a child hospitalized because of physical abuse.

More frequently, however, juvenile court judges handling child welfare cases try to make sure that parents provide for the basic needs and supervision of their children. A typical case might involve a child who has been absent from school for weeks. School authorities would ask the child welfare department to check on the family to see if there is a problem.

"If the family makes no attempt to get the child to school, the case is brought in for a protective custody hearing," said David Bonfiglio, a juvenile court judge in Indiana. "I talk to the parents and explain that state law requires that a child attend school. Then I order attendance except when a doctor or nurse says a child is too ill to be in school. Usually, in such cases, parents do not see the value of education, are young—usually single parents—struggling financially, and may be keeping the child home from school to babysit for a younger sibling."

Judge Bonfiglio pointed out that child welfare workers are required to monitor the family and see that parents comply with the law. Perhaps the worker will refer the parents to parenting classes. Perhaps there is a problem with alcohol or substance abuse.

"The point of the law in all cases is to try to provide services that will help the family function and stay intact," the judge said. He is convinced that early intervention helps prevent more serious family problems, such as child delinquency or abuse of children. "In dealing with delinquent kids, I find that almost all have been abused or neglected when younger, so I feel that had there been protective services for the family, the delinquency might have been prevented," Bonfiglio said.

Varied Roles of Caregivers

The child welfare workers who intervene are perhaps criticized and blamed more than any other caregivers for whatever action they take or do not take. As an Illinois worker put it: "Nobody's happy with you. Birth parents don't like you when you remove their children from their home. Foster parents get upset with you because you have to work within the system. Kids don't trust you because they fear you will add to the pain in their lives."

Clearly, the reports of children being harmed and killed while in the custody of the child welfare system show that some caregivers—like some teachers, doctors, therapists, and others—are negligent or ill equipped to do their jobs. But most child welfare workers are dedicated to protecting kids and finding ways to nurture them. To carry out that task, workers must play a number of roles and perform a variety of duties.

A child welfare worker (or child protective worker, as the person may be called) is usually the one who investigates reports of child maltreatment and determines whether the reports are valid. Some reports may be filed by a person seeking revenge or by someone who has made a mistaken judgment. If a worker must intervene to take a child into protective custody, she or he may have to face hostile parents. Or the worker may have to deal with parents who are out of touch with reality because of alcohol or substance abuse or mental illness. At the same time, a worker must try to assess whether or not it will be possible to bring about change in the family and reunite them.

Child welfare workers also are educators, helping mothers and fathers learn parenting skills. They may have to provide emotional support for children and young people in foster care and for birth and foster parents. They may have to recruit foster and adoptive parents and set up foster/adoptive parent support groups. They may be role models for young people in foster care. They may work with other professionals, such as lawyers and psychiatrists, to determine what actions are in the best interests of children in their custody. They may also help children, teenagers, and parents get in touch with community

Organizations such as the Child Abuse Prevention Services (CAPS) in Elkhart, Indiana, help parents learn parenting skills. CAPS also works with young victims of abuse who often have developmental problems that may be overcome with preschool day treatment programs. About half of the abused children in the CAPS program have been removed from their birth homes and placed in foster care.

groups, self-help networks, educational programs, and other supportive services such as those described in the previous chapter.

Helping foster children get the services they need to live independently is another role of child welfare workers. Some young people who have been adrift in the foster care system for most of their lives have severe and multiple problems. Many are hostile and lack self-esteem. Some are mentally retarded. Others are unable to develop trusting relationships. Most lack daily living and job skills.

In a variety of programs connected with social service agencies, child welfare workers and foster parents work together to help young people "age out" of the foster care system. When successful, young people find and maintain jobs and homes. They also are able to connect with friends or relatives for emotional support, and they learn how to manage their emotions and behavior.

Volunteer Workers

Many groups or organizations that work with and for families are staffed with volunteers as well as paid consultants. For example, in cases of child abuse and neglect, a juvenile court judge may appoint a volunteer to represent a child or family outside the court. The volunteer could be involved in a Court Appointed Special Advocates program. If a child is in foster care, a special advocate visits the foster home to make sure that the child is getting appropriate care. Or if a child has been in foster care for a long time, an advocate checks to see that the child welfare agency is taking steps to free a child for adoption.

Volunteers and professionals in some states take part in citizen review boards. These boards monitor child welfare agencies to see that a plan has been developed for each child who is a ward of the court. The Child Welfare Act of 1980 requires that there be a specific plan for placing a child in a permanent home or for reuniting a child with her or his birth parents. The plan also must include a date for achieving the stated goals.

Many other volunteers work with runaway programs, emergency shelters, and treatment centers that serve young people who are wards of the court or need protective services. People who work to protect infants, children, and teens—whether volunteers or paid staff—can be found in nearly every community. Some can be reached by calling a hotline number. Others are available through such local facilities as schools, police stations, or clinics. In some cases, volunteer helpers can be contacted by letters or phone calls to national or regional organizations.

Of the millions of people involved in efforts to protect children and preserve and strengthen families, most would agree with the first lines of the song "Greatest Love of All" popularized by Whitney Houston. The song says: "I believe that children are our future; teach them well and let them lead the way." But in order for young people to reach their potential and to lead, many need to be assured of safe, healthy, and permanent homes. As Marian Wright Edelman, founder and president of the Children's Defense Fund, which advocates for children, wrote:

> A principal challenge for the next ten years in the U.S., both within and outside of government, must be to mount a carefully conceived, comprehensive human investment effort in all our young and their families. . . . We must begin with a national commitment that ensures that every child has basic health, nutrition, and early childhood services and the opportunity to develop strong basic skills.

Notes and References by Chapter

Besides personal interviews, a variety of published materials provided background for this book. The following source materials were the basis for some of the information presented. Most of the references are self-explanatory; others are briefly annotated to aid anyone interested in further research.

Chapter 1

Adoption Resource Book. A public listing of children waiting for adoption, available in most state and county child welfare offices.

Carey, Ann. "Happy Ending: Sunday's Child Success Story." *South Bend Tribune*, November 22, 1987, pp. S1, S10.

"Sunday's Child." Regular column in Sunday editions of the *South Bend Tribune*, South Bend, Ind.

"Waiting Children." Pages from various editions of newsletters published by Building Families Through Adoption and OURS (addresses listed in "Helpful Organizations").

Chapter 2

Cautley, Patricia Woodward. *New Foster Parents: The First Experience*. New York: Human Sciences Press, 1980.

Kadushin, Alfred. *Child Welfare Services*. Chapter 8, "Substitute Care: Foster Family Care," pp. 313–411.

Mortland, Carol A., and Egan, Maura G. "Vietnamese Youth in American Foster Care." *Social Work*, May–June 1987, pp. 240–245.

The National Advocate. (A bimonthly newsletter of the National Foster Parent Association, which contains articles and letters about foster parenting and foster children and young people.)

O'Dea, Colleen. "Foster Parenting." *Daily Record* (New Jersey), YOU section, pp. 8–10.

Seigel, Jessica. "Church Families Open Hearts to Teens." *Chicago Tribune*, May 6, 1988, Section 1, p. 9.

State of California. *Foster Family Homes: Manual of Policies and Procedures.* Sacramento, Ca.: State of California Health and Welfare Agency, Department of Social Services, 1984.

Villamor, Linda. "Program Provides Haven for Asian Refugees." *New York Times*, April 17, 1988, pp. 1, 27.

Chapter 3

Felker, Evelyn. *Foster Parenting Young Children: Guidelines From a Foster Parent.* Washington, D.C.: Child Welfare League of America, 1974.

Holz, Loretta. *Foster Child.* New York: Julian Messner, 1984. (A story with photographs about what it is like to be a foster child.)

Kantrowitz, Barbara, with King, Patricia. " 'Will You Be My Mother?' "*Newsweek*, May 9, 1988, pp. 74–75.

Rex, Betty, as told to Pierce, Barbara. "The Tears—and Rage—of a Foster Mother."*Redbook*, July 1987, pp. 34, 37.

Rice, Dale L., and McFadden, Emily Jean. "A Forum for Foster Children."*Child Welfare*, May–June 1988, pp. 231–243.

Rose, Leslie. "With Open Arms."*Woman's World*, March 15, 1988, p. 36. (Story about a foster family in Chicago.)

Taft, Philip B. "Love Triumphs on Frazier Street."*Reader's Digest*, December 1986, pp. 130–134. (Story of a couple who set up a foster group home for teenage gang members in Philadelphia).

Chapter 4

Adler, Jack. *Fundamentals of Group Child Care.* Cambridge, Mass.: Ballinger Publishing Company, 1981.

Stepleton, Susan S. "Specialized Foster Care: Families as Treatment Resources." *Children Today*, March–April 1987, pp. 27–31. (Describes comprehensive group care treatment at The Hope Center, St. Louis, Missouri, and the center's therapeutic foster family program.)

Chapter 5

Martin, Cynthia D. *Beating the Adoption Game*. San Diego, New York, London: Harcourt Brace Jovanovich, 1988.

Perlman, Lisa. "Open Adoption Gaining Supporters in Michigan." *Daily Record* (New Jersey), April 17, 1988, p. A11.

Powledge, Fred. *So You're Adopted*. New York: Scribners, 1982.

Stabiner, Karen. "The Baby Brokers." *Los Angeles Times Magazine*, August 14, 1988, pp. 8–16, 35–38.

Chapter 6

Gilman, Lois. *The Adoption Resource Book*. New York: Harper & Row, 1987.

Henig, Robin Marantz. "Chosen and Given." *New York Times Magazine*, September 11, 1988, pp. 70–72. (Describes the "psychological burdens" that adoptees carry.)

Krausman, Susan. " 'Stereotypes' of Adoption Are Inaccurate." *Education Week*, January 31, 1990, p. 32.

Krementz, Jill. *How It Feels to Be Adopted*. New York: Knopf, 1982.

Marcus, Clare. *Who Is My Mother?* Toronto, Canada: Macmillan of Canada, 1981.

Chapter 7

Arcari, M. Teresa, and Betman, Beth Gwinn. "The Deaf Child in Foster Care." *Children Today*, July–August 1986, pp. 17–21.

DeCroce, Tracy. "Finding Homes for AIDS Babies." *Chicago*, April 1988, pp. 14–16.

Foster, Patricia H., and Whitworth, J. M. "Medical Foster Care: An

Alternative to Long-Term Hospitalization." *Children Today*, July–August 1986, pp. 12–16.

Fryxell, David A. "Housefuls of Happy Results." *Friendly Exchange*, February 1986, pp. 23–25. (Describes adoption of special needs kids.)

Laws, Rita. "It's Time to Notice Our Invisible Children." *U.S. News & World Report*, August 10, 1987, p. 4. (An opinion piece on the joys of special needs adoption.)

Chapter 8

Cheslow, Jerry. "State Offers New Program on Adoption of Blacks." *New York Times*, September 11, 1988, pp. 1, 4–6.

The Children's Voice. (A quarterly publication of the National Coalition to End Racism in America's Child Care System; contains articles and letters about cross-racial/cultural adoption and foster care, primarily in the United States.)

Fantini, Mario D., and Cardenas, Rene, eds. *Parenting in a Multicultural Society.* New York: Longman, 1980.

Feigelman, William, and Silverman, Arnold R. "The Long-Term Effects of Transracial Adoption." *Social Service Review*, December 1984, pp. 588–602.

Gay, Kathlyn. *The Rainbow Effect: Interracial Families.* New York: Franklin Watts, 1987.

Ladner, Joyce A. *Mixed Families: Adopting Across Racial Boundaries.* Garden City/New York: Anchor Press/Doubleday, 1978.

OURS: The Magazine of Adoptive Families. (A bimonthly publication that contains articles and letters about cross-racial/cultural adoptions, including many foreign adoptions.)

Simon, Rita., and Altstein, Howard. *Transracial Adoptees and Their Families: A Study of Identity and Commitment.* New York, London: Praeger, 1987.

Warren, Andrea. "Adopting a Foreign Child." *Better Homes and Gardens*, October 1985, pp. 25–27.

Wolfe, Diane C. "A Baby Boom of Foreign Adoptions." *Insight*, October 3, 1988, pp. 36–38.

Chapter 9

Barth, Richard P. "Disruption in Older Child Adoptions." *Public Welfare*, Winter 1988, pp. 23–29.

Bernikow, Louise. "The Children Nobody Wants." *Redbook*, December 1986, pp. 124–126.

"Crimes Against Children: The Failure of Foster Care." ABC News Closeup (TV special and transcript), August 30, 1988.

Harris, Louis. *Inside America*. New York: Vintage Books, 1987.

Hornby, Helaine C. "Why Adoptions Disrupt." *Children Today*, July–August 1986, pp. 7–11.

Janeway, Elizabeth. "Child Care Inc." *World Monitor*, October 1988, pp. 68–73. (Describes how corporate America is learning from other nations how to provide child care for working parents.)

Lueck, Thomas J. "Study Faults Foster-Care Conditions." *New York Times*, September 4, 1988, p. 34.

McCormick, John. "America's Third World." *Newsweek*, August 8, 1988, pp. 20–24. (Describes the plight of the nation's rural poor.)

Moynihan, Daniel Patrick. *Family and Nation*. San Diego, New York, London: Harcourt Brace Jovanovich, 1987.

Papajohn, George. "Boy Raped in Shelter Run by State." *Chicago Tribune*, May 9, 1988, Section 2, pp. 1–2.

Quinn, Jane Bryant. "A Crisis in Child Care." *Newsweek*, February 15, 1988, p. 57.

Seligson, Tom. "Who Speaks for the Lost Children?: A Report on Foster Care in America." *Parade*, July 31, 1988, pp. 4–7.

Smith, Dinitia. "Children of the Night: New York's Foster-Care Crisis." *New York*, December 1, 1986, pp. 81–100.

Smith, Kathleen, and Reder, Nancy. "Meeting Basic Human Needs: A Crisis of Responsibility." A report from the League of Women Voters Education Fund, 1987.

Sullivan, Cheryl. "America's Troubled Children: Wards of the State." *Christian Science Monitor*, September 27, 1988, pp. B1–B8.

Tumposky, Ellen. "Little People, Big Risk: Babies in Care of City." *Daily News*, May 1, 1988, pp. 7, 49.

Van Gelder, Lindsy, and Brandt, Pam. "How Foster Care Is Failing Our Children." *McCall's*, March 1988, pp. 82–85.

Weiss, Stefanie. "No Place Called Home." *NEA Today*, September 1988, pp. 10–11.

Chapter 10

AuClaire, Philip, and Schwartz, Ira M. "Are Home Based Services Effective?" *Children Today*, May–June 1987, pp. 6–9.

Children Today. Special Issue: Family Based Services. November–December 1986.

Kagan, Sharon L.; Powell, Douglas R.; Weissbourd, Bernice; and Zigler, Edward F., eds. *America's Family Support Programs*. New Haven and London: Yale University Press, 1987.

Maluccio, Anthony N., and Sinanoglu, Paula A., eds. *The Challenge of Partnership: Working With Parents of Children in Foster Care*. New York: Child Welfare League of America, 1980.

Proch, Kathleen, and Howard, Jeanne A. "Parental Visiting of Children in Foster Care." *Social Work*, May–June 1986, pp. 178–181.

Your Child in Foster Care: What Happens and Where Do You Go From Here? 1983. (A handbook for parents published by the Indianapolis Bar Association as part of an American Bar Association Law and Child Protection Project.)

Chapter 11

Adler, Jerry, and Drew, Lisa. "Saving the Children." *Newsweek*, January 25, 1988, pp. 58–59.

Besharov, Douglas J. *The Vulnerable Social Worker*. Silver Spring, Maryland: National Association of Social Workers, 1985.

(Describes how social workers can be blamed for whatever they
do and discusses the liabilities social workers face.)

"How to Help Kids in Crisis." *Modern Maturity*, August–September
1988, p. 13.

Jacoby, Tamar, with Springen, Karen and Lazarovici, Laureen. "Is
Sterilization the Answer?" *Newsweek*, August 8, 1988, p. 59.

Kantrowitz, Barbara, with King, Patricia; Witherspoon, Deborah; and
Barrett, Todd. "How to Protect Abused Children." *Newsweek*,
November 23, 1987, pp. 70–71.

McLeod, Beverly. "Fostering Mentally Healthy Children."
Psychology Today, January 1985, p. 18.

Maidman, Frank, ed. *Child Welfare: A Source Book of Knowledge and
Practice*. New York: Child Welfare League of America, 1984.

Monmaney, Terence. "When Abortion Is Denied." *Newsweek*, August
22, 1988, p. 64.

Tumposky, Ellen. "Foster Program Keeping Families United." *Daily
News*, August 28, 1988, p. 29.

Note: A catalog describing many books and other materials on
adoption, foster care, and child protective services is available from
The Child Welfare League of America, Publications Department, 440
First Street, NW, Suite 310, Washington, DC 20001.

Further Reading

Cohen, Shari, *Coping with Being Adopted*. New York: Rosen Group, 1988.

DuPrau, Jeanne. *Adoption: The Facts, Feelings & Issues of a Double Heritage*. New York: Messner, 1981.

Gay, Kathlyn. *Changing Families*. Hillside, N.J.: Enslow Publishers, 1988.

Nickman, Steven L. *The Adoption Experiences*. New York: Messner, 1985.

Powledge, Fred. *So You're Adopted*. New York: Macmillan, 1982.

Scott, Elaine. *Adoption*. New York: Watts, 1980.

Helpful Organizations

Aask America
1540 Market Street
San Francisco, CA 94102

Adoptees Anonymous
P.O. Box 1795
Winnipeg, Manitoba
Canada

Adoptees Liberty Movement Association
P.O. Box 154
Washington Bridge Station
New York, NY 10033

Adoptive Families of America
3307 Highway 100 N, Suite 203
Minneapolis, MN 55422

Al-Anon Family Group Headquarters
One Park Avenue
New York, NY 10016

Alcoholics Anonymous
P.O. Box 459
Grand Central Station
New York, NY 10163

Americans for International Adoption
877 S. Adams, Suite 106
Birmingham, MI 48011

Big Brothers/Big Sisters of America
230 N. 13th Street
Philadelphia, PA 19107

Building Families Through Adoption
P.O. Box 550
Dawson, MN 56232

Catholic Social Service
222 N. 17th Street
Philadelphia, PA 19103

Children's Bureau
U.S. Department of Health and Human Services
P.O. Box 1182
Washington, DC 20013

Children's Defense Fund
122 C Street NW
Washington, DC 20001

Child Welfare League of
America
440 First St. NW, Suite 310
Washington, DC 20001

Committee for Single
Adoptive Parents
P.O. Box 15084
Chevy Chase, MD 20815

Family Service America
44 E. 23rd Street
New York, NY 10010

Foster Parents Plan
International
Box 80
East Greenwich, RI 02818

Holt International Children's
Services
P.O. Box 2880
Eugene, OR 94702

Indian Rights Association
1505 Race Street
Philadelphia, PA 19102

National Center for Juvenile
Justice
701 Forbes Avenue
Pittsburgh, PA 15219

National Center for the
Prevention and Treatment of
Child Abuse and Neglect
University of Colorado Medical
Center
1205 Oneida Street
Denver, CO 80220

National Coalition to End
Racism in America's Child
Care System, Inc.
22075 Koths
Taylor, MI 48180

National Committee for the
Prevention of Child Abuse
332 S. Michigan Avenue
Suite 1250
Chicago, IL 60604

National Foster Parent
Association
226 Kilts Drive
Houston, TX 77024

National Mental Health
Association
1021 Prince Street
Alexandria, VA 22314-2971

National Network of
Runaway and Youth Services
905 6th Street SW, No. 411B
Washington, DC 20004

Native American Adoption Resource Exchange
c/o Council of Three Rivers
American Indian Center
200 Charles Street
Dorseyville, PA 15238

North American Council on Adoptable Children
P.O. Box 14808
Minneapolis, MN 55414

Parenting for Peace & Justice
4144 Lindell Boulevard
St. Louis, MO 63108

Parents Anonymous
22330 Hawthorne Boulevard
Suite 208
Torrance, CA 90505

Treatment Foster Care Association
1215 N. Augusta Street
Staunton, VA 24401

WAIF
67 Irving Place
New York, NY 10003

Index